ESSAYS ON THE
POLITICAL ECONOMY

ESSAYS ON THE POLITICAL ECONOMY

JAMES M. BUCHANAN

UNIVERSITY OF HAWAII PRESS / HONOLULU

94 93 92 91 90 89 5 4 3 2 1

Library of Congress Cataloging-in-Publication Data

Buchanan, James M.
  Essays on the political economy / James M. Buchanan.
    p. cm.
  ISBN 0-8248-1250-6
  1. Economics. 2. Free enterprise. 3. Social choice.
4. Constitutional law. 5. Economic policy. I. Title.
  HB71.B7794   1989   89-4690
  338.9—dc19   CIP

∞ *The paper used in this publication meets the minimum
requirements of American National Standard for Information
Sciences—Permanence of Paper for Printed Library Materials*
                                      ANSI Z39.48-1984

Chapter 3 was adapted from convocation exercises at
North Carolina State University in October 1988. Chapter 4 was presented at the Southern Economic Association Meeting in November 1987. Chapter 7 was
reprinted with permission of *Banca Nazionale del Lavoro
Quarterly Review,* No. 159, December 1986.

These essays are collected
and published in memory of
H. Laurence Miller, Jr., professor
of economics at the University
of Hawaii and member of the
faculty editorial board of the
University of Hawaii Press, by
his friends and colleagues

CONTENTS

FOREWORD

James M. Buchanan is one of the world's most eminent economists. He is a Distinguished Fellow of the American Economic Association, and, in 1986, received the Nobel Memorial Prize in Economic Science for his contributions to public finance, political economy, and the theory of public choice. He is also one of the most original, prescient, and controversial of contemporary economists.

Among American economists of his stature, Buchanan's roots are unique in being rural and Southern. He was born near Murfreesboro in Tennessee in 1919, and was educated on the farm, at home, and in rural schools before graduating from Middle Tennessee State Teachers College and the University of Tennessee. During the Second World War, Buchanan was an officer of the U.S. Navy and spent three years on the staff of Admiral Nimitz at Pearl Harbor, first as an operations watch officer and later as assistant operations officer, helping to keep the running record of the deployment of naval forces in the Pacific. After the war, Buchanan had an option of staying on for a career in the navy or returning to university for graduate work. He chose the latter, and in 1948 received a Ph.D. in economics from the University of Chicago, where he was a student of Frank H. Knight.

Four of the seven essays collected in this volume derive from talks given by Professor Buchanan on a return to Oahu in March 1988 at the invitation of the Department of Economics of the University of Hawaii, Manoa. The lead essay of this collection on the political economy is based on a public lecture at the university. The political economy of the budget deficit is a subject upon which Buchanan has been most prescient. Since the mid-1950s he has predicted with singular courage that the postwar theory of macroeconomic policy, when placed in the context of majoritarian politics, could be a recipe for unconscionable wastage of revenues by popular representatives, naturally looking to maintain themselves in office by serving the interests of their constituents. It is this broad observation that led Buchanan first into the theory of "public choice," an introduction to which is found in the second essay collected here, and more recently into "constitutional political economy," discussed in the third and fourth essays.

The first of these avenues may be summarily described as an application of the economic principles of rational pursuit of individual interest and exchange to diverse contexts within majoritarian politics. The second reflects Buchanan's enduring concern with the future—specifically, that the forces of majoritarian politics are such that all too often the future can come to be discounted too rapidly in favor of present consumption. Buchanan's view has been that, in the absence of more traditional and implicit forms of self-discipline such as ethical or religious codes of conduct, an explicit fiscal and monetary constitution may be the only practicable means to inducing a longer-term outlook on majoritarian legislatures.

If a single consistent theme is to be found in Buchanan's work in public economics, it is with his concern with the future and the longer term. Thus, the first four essays of this book may be seen as comprising a whole, being quite a good representation of Buchanan's thinking on the subject which has concerned him most.

The remaining three essays are instructive for somewhat different reasons. In the few pages of the fifth essay on the nature of the work ethic, Buchanan argues that economists (perhaps since Karl Marx) may have erred in the way they have characterized work and leisure. He takes issue, in this brief essay, with the view that work and leisure produce disutility and utility, that is, that labor is a commodity like any other. Buchanan suggests that there are aspects of work that surely produce pleasure and aspects of leisure that surely do not. In the next essay on the open economy, Buchanan looks at why coalitions of rent-seeking producer groups may tend to be unstable, given the complicated interdependence between production processes in which inputs of one industry can be outputs of another. He argues that this instability may explain, in part, why we do not see more protectionism than we do. Finally, there is a reflective autobiographical essay that traces the milestones of his intellectual history prior to winning the Nobel Prize.

There may be something less than obvious in these three essays that may bear to be remarked upon. Among many whom he has befriended, Buchanan is known to command a quite fierce loyalty and dedication. These include people from all walks of life, poor and rich, educated and not. The final essay of this volume, which speaks of Buchanan's roots, will to an extent explain the source of this loyalty. Buchanan has been and remains close to the simplicity and equality that binds rural communities together. He is, in this sense, very much an egalitarian in outlook, and is in fact severely unpretentious and antielitist. It is this which allows him, for example, to admit to graduate students or young colleagues or even to a public audience that he is perplexed by a problem or at a total impasse and needs their help, or to float admittedly incomplete ideas in order to see whether they do or do not deserve to be completed. The fifth and sixth essays may be seen as examples of this kind of intellectual experimentation.

Among the most pressing economic concerns facing the new administration in Washington, and for that matter the administration which will follow it four years from now, is the question of how to treat the budget deficit in a sensible way. It might be safely assumed that the problem is a highly complicated and multifaceted one, and that plausible and realistic solutions are not going to be

easily available. The role of the academic economist is quite different from that of the statesman or the politician. Perhaps its most
important aspect is to contribute to the discussion in an independent way, and as candidly and clearly as possible. On the vitally
important subject of the national deficit and the public debt, and the
questions which stem therefrom, James Buchanan has sought for
forty years to do precisely that. It is hoped that this slim collection
of essays will serve to give the interested general reader an indica-
tion of his contribution.

SUBROTO ROY

1. THE POLITICAL ECONOMY OF THE BUDGET DEFICIT

Introduction

My IDEAS on the economics and the politics of debt-financed budgetary deficits are not widely accepted by my fellow economists. Indeed, my thinking on the subject may be much closer to that emerging from the common sense of the ordinary citizen. These ideas were initially presented in my 1958 book *Public Principles of Public Debt,* which challenged the then-orthodox Keynesian notion that public debt involves no temporal shift of burden because "we owe it to ourselves." My basic beliefs have not changed over the course of three decades; but the importance of the subject matter has changed. It is far more important in the late 1980s than it was in the 1950s to get the fundamentals of the analysis correct. My second major effort was a book, *Democracy in Deficit,* written jointly with Richard E. Wagner and published in 1978. This second book did not examine the economic consequences of debts and deficits; it instead tried to explain why modern or post-Keynesian democratic decision processes generate quasipermanent deficit financing. Whereas the first book was an attack on the Keynesian macroeconomic theory of public debt, the second book was an attack on the Keynesian presuppositions about democratic politics.

It is perhaps not surprising that my efforts in both cases ruffled the feathers of economists, who remain dominated by the macroeconomic paradigm imposed by the mid-century Keynesian "revolution" in economic thinking. I shall not continue my ongoing argument with other economists in this context, but some mention of my adversary stance is helpful as background for the subsequent discussion.

The Elementary Principles

In the simplest terms, the economic consequences of a debt-financed budgetary deficit are equivalent to the economic consequences of a debt-financed deficit in the account of any economic-financial unit, whether this be a person, a family, a corporation, a club, a church, or a labor union. When current revenues fall short of current outlays or expenditures, a deficit emerges, and if revenues are not increased or outlays decreased, the deficit or shortfall must be financed by borrowing. (With national governments, which possess money-creation authority, budget deficits may also be financed directly by money issue. I shall leave this possible revenue source out of the discussion here, since the relevant subject matter involves the consequences of debt-financed deficits. These consequences may in themselves make some ultimate resort to monetization more likely, a point I shall touch on briefly below.)

For both the borrower and the lender, the sale and purchase of debt instruments involves a temporal displacement in the availability of funds. The borrower is enabled to spend more than revenue or income in the initial budgetary period, but is obliged to spend less than revenue or income in some future period. The lender, on the other hand, spends less than revenue or income in the initial period but is enabled to spend more than revenue or income in periods during which the debt is amortized. And, as I have argued for three decades, the government is not fundamentally different in these respects from any other borrower.

A return to the primer is required because of the immense confusion in much of the discussion of public debt and deficits. If we rule out default for the time being, the primary economic consequence of debt-financed spending by government is the guaranteed necessity that we must, as citizens-taxpayers-program beneficiaries, give up some part of our incomes in future periods in order to meet interest and amortization charges on debt. A share of our future incomes is obligated to meet the legitimate claims held by creditors of the government. And it makes no difference whatsoever whether these creditors are themselves citizens or foreigners.

The financing of current government spending by debt is equivalent to an "eating up" of our national capital value. If we define a capital value by discounting an expected stream of future incomes, then any offset against such future incomes reduces this value. And it does so in precisely the same way that consumption of a capital asset would. By financing current public outlay by debt, we are, in effect, chopping up the apple trees for firewood, thereby reducing the yield of the orchard forever.

The analogy between debt-financed public consumption and the destruction of capital value is often rejected because, it is argued, with internal debt held by citizens, the obligations against future incomes embodied in public debt are just matched by the claims held by those who have purchased the government's securities. In this simplistic macroeconomic logic, there is no effect on capital values summed over the economy. The absurdity of this argument is demonstrated once we recognize that those who purchase the securities do so in a wholly voluntary exchange transaction, and that, precisely because the purchase is voluntary, these same persons might have used the funds either to purchase other income-yielding private assets or for initial-period private consumption. In either case, the capital values of claims held by those who purchase the government securities cannot be counted as positive offsets to the negative capital value that is necessarily embodied in the obligation to meet future interest and amortization charges.

This negative value is a charge against the portfolio of citizens, as members of the political unit, and it is not matched by any offsetting positive increment to the capital value appropriately assigned to this same portfolio. This result holds quite independently of the sources of the initial funds loaned to government.

Domestic and Foreign Debt

This basic logical error in analysis informs the familiar argument that debt claims held by foreigners, so-called external debt, is more onerous than debt claims held by citizens or domestic organizations. The error here stems from a failure to consider the alternatives initially faced by the purchasers of securities. If debt instruments are bought by citizens, alternative uses of funds in the domestic economy are foreclosed. If the bonds are bought by foreigners, these alternatives in the domestic economy remain open. The claims against future income held by foreigners in the second case are precisely equivalent to the value of the uses of the funds that remain available for exploitation in either private investment or consumption opportunities. As citizens, as members of the political organization of government, we are in exactly the same position whether the national debt is held by persons inside or outside of the national economy.

It is often suggested that the 1980s regime of massive deficits has been sustainable without major economic damage only because foreigners have purchased large blocs of the securities issued to finance the deficits. Otherwise, it is suggested, budget deficits of the magnitude experienced would have exerted unacceptable upward pressures in interest rates. My conclusion about the equivalent effects of foreign and domestic debt does not contradict such a suggestion. The impact of a debt-financed deficit of any given size on the rate of interest will depend on the supply of loanable funds, and if foreign investors supply funds for domestic loan markets, public or private, the rate of interest will be lower than it would be if such foreign investment funds were not made available. It makes no difference at all whether foreigners purchase private or governmental securities.

Crowding Out

A second major source of confusion, or at the least of ambiguity, involves the "crowding out" issue. Since debt financing requires government to *sell* securities in exchange for funds supplied by lenders, funds that are then used up when government spends, it seems evident that these funds might have been used by the lenders to purchase income-yielding private claims. Prospective sellers of private securities (for example, firms seeking to expand capital facilities by floating new issues of stocks or bonds) are "crowded out." Private securities can be marketed only at interest rates that are much higher than those which would prevail in the absence of the government borrowing operation.

This seemingly straightforward argument has been challenged by some economists, who suggest that the issue of public debt, in itself, stimulates new savings. According to this argument, citizens will recognize the future-period tax liabilities that are embodied in any issue of public debt. They will accordingly adjust their behavior so that these future tax payments, which will be imposed either on themselves or their descendants, can be more easily met. In this scenario, the citizen, who can and will observe government borrowing, will put aside additional savings by reducing current rates of consumption spending. The additional saving will, to the extent that it takes place, match the additional demands on loanable funds that the public borrowing operation represents. In the limit, if the new saving offset is complete, there is no "crowding out." And, even if not complete, any new saving generated as a result of public debt issue will make the crowding out of private capital formation less than the initial argument might suggest.

My own position is that whether or not debt financing of budget deficits "crowds out" private investment and capital formation is essentially a secondary rather than a primary consequence. By labeling this issue to be secondary, I am not suggesting that it is unimportant. I am suggesting instead that economists' undue concentration on this question, to the almost total neglect of the more important primary effect or consequence of debt, is inexcusable. In order to emphasize my position, let me, strictly for the purposes of discussion here, assume that no crowding out occurs at all. Assume that there is no effect of debt-financed deficits on the rate of interest, and hence on the rate of capital formation in the economy. This result would require that new savings are generated just sufficient to finance fully all of government's debt instruments offered.

The primary *economic* consequence of debt-financed deficits would still be present even in this extreme and totally unrealistic case. There will be a net claim against future private income flows in the economy, a claim held by creditors of the government, all those persons, individuals or organizations, domestic or foreign, who hold government securities. Taxes, which are by their very nature coercive, must be levied against persons in order to generate the revenues that are required to finance the interest charges on the debt. That share of private incomes that must be devoted to tax payments cannot, by definition, be available for private disposition as individuals might desire, acting in either their private or their public capacities. The burden of having to make the tax payments from personal income streams will be present, quite independently of the behavior of those who make the initial-period decisions as to how much to save and to consume. The person who is faced with a tax bill to finance interest charges will not make any relationship between the saving that his or her parents may or may not have made because the debt was issued earlier. The person faced with such a tax bill will reckon only on the simply observed fact that income that he or she might otherwise use is being taken away in taxes. The result is precisely analogous to the apple orchard example introduced earlier. If the yield of three trees under a person's nominal ownership is committed to debt service, it is fully equivalent to having an orchard with three fewer trees.

How Long Can We Tax the Future?

The descriptive implications of the elementary analysis are clear. The federal government has embarked on a debt-financed spending spree that cannot be permanently sustained. The fact that the government cannot go bankrupt in any sense analogous to a person or business firm does nothing to modify the central proposition. Government's ultimate taxing and money-creation powers can, of course, guarantee that all nominally valued debt claims will be honored, but neither an everincreasing interest share of tax revenues nor an inflationary monetization of nominal debt claims offers a viable option for permanent reform.

The budgetary deficit must be reduced. But what are the consequences of this reduction? Current rates of government spending must be cut back, perhaps dramatically, and/or current rates of tax must be increased, perhaps dramatically. Either of these steps, or any combination of the two, must also have serious economic consequences. Spending cuts will reduce expected benefits to all those persons and groups that have come to anticipate continued program expansions. Tax increases will reduce incomes available for private disposition by individuals, some share of which would be devoted to private investment.

A reduction in the deficit, financed by either a cut in rates of government spending or an increase in rates of tax, could be predicted to somewhat lower the rate of interest, because the reduction in government's demand for loanable funds would not be fully off-set by a reduction in the supply of such funds. This effect on the rate of interest is again a secondary consequence of the reduction of elimination of the deficit. The primary consequence is the shift of the incidence of payment for government programs from future-period taxpayers to those taxpayers who are around during the period when the government outlays are actually made.

At some point, this shift in the temporal incidence of government spending must be made. Real growth in the national economy can postpone the day of reckoning, but interest charges cannot permanently take up an increasing share of the federal budget.

Do We Need to Change the Rules?

But is there much prospect that our democratic decision procedures will accomplish this shift in incidence? Must we not predict that these processes will operate to insure that the deficit dilemma gets much worse before it gets better? Having embarked on the debt-financed spending spree, will our political structure, as it is currently organized, measure up to the challenge that it faces?

I do not think that it can do so—or will do so. As we can all observe, there seem to be almost insurmountable political costs involved in either spending cuts or tax increases. Modern American politics operates in accordance with a set of rules that makes effective resolution of the deficit issue almost impossible. The implication of this should be clear. Improvement or reform can only be expected to occur if the rules are changed. It is on this conviction that I have long been a strong supporter of proposals for a constitutional amendment to require budget balance.

I shall not develop the argument for such an amendment here. I have done that many times before, and that is not my present assignment. I want instead to take a "realistic" perspective and to examine what seems now, in the late 1980s, to be the most probable scenario. Regardless of what I might personally hope for, I do not now predict enactment of an enforceable balanced-budget amendment to the constitution within the next decade. Further, I do not think that congressional precommitments in the general Gramm-Rudman form will prove effective. There may well be quasisuccessful short-run congressional attempts to reduce the size of the budget deficits without changes in the basic decision procedures or rules. These efforts may, however, actually be counterproductive over the long term because they may, to the extent that they are successful in the short term, serve merely to distract attention from the structural-procedural reform that is required. Any such short-term congressional restoration of effective fiscal discipline could be and probably would be dissipated rapidly by return to fiscal profligacy. Recognizing this prospect, why should political leaders incur both political and economic costs now for the benefit of political leaders and constituents who come along later?

Prospects for Default

What, then, can we realistically expect? Continued expressions of concern about debt-financed deficits with little observed success in doing much about them? Mounting interest charges that consume larger and larger shares in federal budgetary outlay?

At some point in such a sequence, default or repudiation of the national debt must become a central political issue. Since the United States national debt is almost exclusively denominated in dollars, the real value of this debt can be reduced dramatically, in the limit to zero, by money issue. There are two ways that default through monetization might take place. First, the Federal Reserve monetary authority could simply purchase all outstanding government securities with newly created dollars. In this setting, all creditors would be guaranteed full nominal values of their claims. The inflation generated by the new money issue would reduce the real values of all fixed claims in the economy; the operation would be equivalent to a tax on all holders of such claims. Alternatively, the monetary authority could generate inflation by issuing additional money through ordinary channels, and in this way reduce the real values of all nominal debt claims outstanding, public and private. The effects would be almost equivalent to the first operation: the effective incidence will be on all holders of fixed claims. The second of these operations is more likely to take place than the first, and with accompanying denials by all concerned that there is any explicit intent to default on the national debt.

The relationship between national debt and another round of inflation deserves somewhat closer attention. Inflation will act to reduce the real value of national debt outstanding; the debt as a share of GNP might level off and even fall. For this reason, all comparisons between sizes of national debt and GNP are highly suspect, since the ratio of debt to product can be reduced dramatically by massive inflation. Such a policy thrust must, however, prove much less effective (from the government's perspective) in the late 1980s and early 1990s than it did in the 1970s. Outstanding debt is now more concentrated in short-term issues, and inflationary expectations would very quickly be incorporated into interest rates. As the government attempts to roll over and refinance maturing issues of debt, interest charges would rise to match the anticipated inflation. The apparently beneficial fiscal results would be largely short term in nature.

As some point in the sequence, more explicit repudiation of the national debt would surely enter into political discussion. And the failure of almost all commentators on the deficits, including economists, to examine seriously debt repudiation seems to me analogous to whistling past the graveyard. When we do consider default seriously, the arguments against such a drastic policy change are not nearly so strong or self-evident as many of us might hope. I cannot here fully develop these arguments on either side, but let me put the question as follows: Why should taxpayers-beneficiaries who live in the year 2000 be coerced into paying for the public program benefits that we, as taxpayers-beneficiaries in the 1980s, have used up? Why should these future-period taxpayers (which may, of course, include many of us) pay for the spending spree? I have looked at this question in some detail, and the strongest argument I can find against default lies in the acknowledged legitimacy of the claims held by the creditors. Those who are purchasing the government securities, and who have purchased them in the past, do and have done so in the expectation that their claims will be honored. To repudiate such claims could amount to a violation of contract, and we like to live in a legal system in which contracts are honored. But governments have often broken contracts before, and, when all is said here, with whom did the creditors contract? I do not want to suggest that the arguments in favor of repudiation of the national debt will become politically dominant. I do suggest that default will become increasingly discussable as the debt-financed spending spree continues.

Default would, of course, call a halt to new borrowing, at least for a time, since lenders would become quite scarce. Note, however, that repudiation of the debt would eliminate the large interest component in the budget. Hence, once we get past the threshold point where the annual interest charges exceed the annual deficit (which is not far off), it will actually be in the short-term interest of current-period taxpayers-beneficiaries to default.

Conclusions

Both our fiscal and our monetary structures are currently in disarray. As members of the body politic, we are all behaving irresponsibly in our unwillingness to look at, analyze, and ultimately to support structural reforms that offer the only prospects for permanent improvement. We have allowed a quasiindependent monetary authority accidentally to attain a monopoly over fiat money issue without effective market or political control. Who can predict a random walk, which is the best modern characterization of the sort of monetary system we endure? Alongside this random-walk monetary authority, we have a fiscal structure from which almost all pretense of balancing off the costs of taxes against the benefits of spending has been removed. The problem is not, however, with irresponsible political leaders, either in the executive or legislative branches of government. The problem is that the rules of the game are such as to make fiscal responsibility and fiscal prudence beyond the limits of the politically feasible. Constituents enjoy the benefits of public spending; they do not enjoy paying taxes. The politics of the deficit is as simple as that.

The tragedy is that so many of us recognize full well what is happening and remain powerless to do anything about it. I have often called for a genuine "constitutional revolution," but how can we move toward its realization?

Let me finish, however, on a somewhat more optimistic note. The proposed amendment for budget balance has been seriously discussed for a decade, and at relevant political levels. Gramm-Rudman at least expresses a recognition of the necessity of fiscal precommitment of some variety. Economists, finally, may be coming around to examination of basic structural changes in our economic and political institutions, and notably in our monetary and fiscal structure. These are all probably necessary precursors to reform in fiscal and monetary rules. If, and this is a big if, we can only get on with such reform before it is too late.

2. THE PUBLIC-CHOICE PERSPECTIVE

Introduction

ON SEVERAL different occasions in recent years, I have offered my interpretation of the history, development, and content of the field of public choice. The very word "perspective" in the title here is helpful in allowing me to get some focus on the general remarks I want to make.

Let me commence by saying what the public-choice perspective is not. It is not a "method" in the usual meaning of the term; that is, it is not a set of tools, nor is it a particular application of standard tools with standard methods, although we are getting somewhat closer with this last statement. Public choice is a *perspective* on politics that emerges from an extension and application of the tools and methods of the economist to collective or nonmarket decision-making. But this statement, in itself, is inadequately descriptive, because, in order to attain such a perspective on politics, a particular approach to economics is required. I shall refer in the following discussion to two separate and distinct aspects of elements in the public-choice perspective. The first aspect is the generalized "catallactics" approach to economics. The second is the more familiar *homo economicus* postulate concerning individual behavior. These two elements, as I shall try to demonstrate, enter with differing weights in the several strands of public-choice theory, inclusively defined.

Catallaxy, or Economics as the Science of Exchanges

What should economists do? My response to this question has been and is: to urge that we exorcise the maximizing paradigm from its dominant place in our tool kit; that we quit defining our discipline, our science, in terms of the scarcity constraint; that we change the very definition, indeed even the very name of our science; that we stop worrying so much about the allocation of resources and the efficiency thereof; and, in place of this whole set of ideas, that we commence concentrating on the origins, properties, and institutions of *exchange,* broadly considered. Adam Smith's propensity to truck and barter one thing for another becomes the proper starting point of our research and inquiry.

The approach to economics that I have long urged and am urging here was called by some nineteenth-century proponents "catallactics," the science of exchanges. More recently, Professor Hayek has suggested the term "catallaxy," which he claims is more in keeping with the proper Greek origins of the word. This approach to economics, as the subject matter for inquiry, draws our attention directly to the *process* of exchange, trade, or agreement to contract. And it necessarily introduces, quite early, the principle of spontaneous order or spontaneous coordination, which is, as I have often suggested, perhaps the only real principle in economic theory as such.

I could of course go on with an elaboration and defense of this approach to economic theory, but such is not my assignment here. It may well be asked what this methodological argument has to do with the public-choice perspective, which is my assignment. My response is straightforward. If we take the catallactics approach seriously, we then quite naturally bring into the analysis complex as well as simple exchange, with complex exchange being defined as that contractual agreement process that goes beyond the economist's magic number "2," beyond the simple two-person, two-commodity barter setting. The emphasis shifts, directly and immediately, to all processes of voluntary agreement among persons.

From this shift in perspective on what economics should be all about, there follows immediately a natural distinction between "economics" as a discipline and "political science" or "politics." There are no lines to be drawn at the edges of "the economy" and "the polity," or between "markets" and "governments," between "the private sector" and "the public sector." Economists need not restrict their inquiries to the behavior of persons within markets, to buying and selling activities as such. By a more or less natural extension of the catallactic approach, economists can look on politics, and on political process, in terms of the exchange paradigm. So long as collective action is modeled with individual decision-makers as the basic units, and so long as such collective action is fundamentally conceived to reflect complex exchange or agreement among all members of a relevant community of persons, such action or behavior or choice may readily be brought under the umbrella of catallaxy. There is no "economists' imperialism," as such, in this inclusion. But there remains a categorical distinction between "economics-as-catallaxy" and "political science" or "politics." The latter, that is, politics as an academic research discipline, is then assigned the whole realm of *nonvoluntary* relations among persons, those relationships involving power or coercion. Interestingly enough, this dividing line between the two areas of social science inquiry is the same as that proposed by some political scientists and sociologists, for example, Talcott Parsons.

Almost any observed empirical relationship among persons will incorporate some catallactic and some power elements. The idealized setting of perfect competition is defined in part for the very purpose of allowing a description of a situation in which there is no power or one person over another at all. In the world where each and every buyer of each and every commodity and service confronts many sellers among whom he may shift costlessly and where each and every seller of each and every commodity or service confronts many buyers among whom he may shift costlessly, there is no power of one person over another. In such a setting, "economic power" becomes totally without meaning or content.

As we depart from this conceptualized ideal, however, as *rents*, actual or potential, emerge in the relationships between and among persons, elements of power and potential coercion arise, and behavior becomes amenable to analysis by something other than pure catallaxy. I do not propose to elaborate on the myriad institutional variants in which both exchange and power elements coexist. I make the categorical distinction largely to suggest that the perspective of economics-as-catallaxy, with its quite natural extension to institutional settings in which persons interact collectively, offers one way of looking at politics and governmental processes, a "different window," to use Nietzchze's metaphor. And, in a very broad sense, this is what the public-choice perspective on politics is about —a different way of looking at the political process, different in kind from that way of looking which emerges from the politics-as-power perspective.

Note that in applying the catallaxy perspective to politics, or in applying public choice, to use the more familiar term, we need not and indeed should not make the mistake of implying, inferring, or suggesting that the power elements of political relationships are squeezed out as if by some methodological magic. The public-choice perspective, which does model politics ultimately on the exchange paradigm, is not necessarily offering an empirically refutable set of hypotheses to the effect that politics and political process is exclusively or even mainly reducible to complex exchange, contract, and agreement. It should be evident that elements of pure rent, and hence of power, emerge more readily in settings of complex than of simple exchange, and hence more readily in many-person that in two-person relationships, in political than in marketlike arrangements. Hence, an appropriate division of scientific labor would call upon the discipline of political science to concentrate more attention on political arrangements and for that of economics to concentrate more attention on market arrangements. There are nonetheless major contributions to be made by the extensions of both perspectives across the whole spectrum of institutions. In this sense, the public-choice perspective on politics becomes analogous to the economic-power perspective on markets.

There are important normative implications to be derived from the public-choice perspective on politics, implications that in turn carry with them an approach to institutional reform. To the extent that voluntary exchange among persons is valued positively while coercion is valued negatively, there emerges the implication that substitution of the former for the latter is desired, presuming, of course, that such substitution is technologically feasible and is not prohibitively costly in resources. This implication provides the normative thrust for the proclivity of the public-choice economist to favor marketlike arrangements where these seem feasible, and to favor decentralization of political authority in appropriate situations.

Even without the normative implications, however, the public-choice perspective on politics directly draws attention to an approach to reform that does emerge from the power perspective. To the extent that political interactions among persons are modeled as a complex exchange process, in which the inputs are individual evaluations or preferences and the process itself is conceived as the means through which these possibly diverging preferences are somehow combined or amalgamated into a pattern or outcomes, attention is more or less necessarily drawn to the interaction process itself rather than to some transcendental evaluation of the outcomes themselves. How does one "improve" a market? One does so by facilitating the exchange process, by reorganizing the rules of trade, contract, or agreement. One does not "improve" or "reform" a marketlike exchange process by an arbitrary rearrangement of final outcomes.

The constitutional perspective, which I have been so closely associated with, emerges naturally from the politics-as-exchange paradigm or research program. To improve politics, it is necessary to improve or reform the rules, the framework within which the game of politics is played. There is no suggestion that improvement lies in the selection of morally superior agents who will use their powers in some "public interest." A game is described by its rules, and a better game is produced only by changing the rules. It is this constitutional perspective, as it emerges from the more inclusive public-choice perspective, that brings public choice into closest contact with current policy issues in the 1980s. I have as an economist always felt uneasy about proffering advice on particular policies, for example, this or that proposed change in the tax law. On the other hand, and by contrast, I do feel it to be within the potential competence of the economist to analyze alternative constitutional regimes or sets of rules and to discuss the predicted workings of alternative constitutional arrangements. Hence, I have been personally, both indirectly and directly, involved in the various proposals for constitutional change that have been made in the seventies and early eighties, like Propositions 1 and 13 in California in 1973 and 1978, respectively (the one unsuccessful the other successful), and Proposition 2 ½ in Massachusetts, and Proposition 6 in Michigan. And, at the federal government level, to the proposed balanced-budget amendment, and to the accompanying tax limit or spending limit proposals, as well as to proposed changes in the basic monetary regime.

Let me return to the suggestion made above to the effect that the public-choice perspective leads directly to attention and emphasis on rules, on constitutions, on constitutional choice, on choice among rules. *The Calculus of Consent* (1962) was the first attempt to derive what Gordon Tullock and I called an "economic theory of political constitutions." It would, of course, have been impossible to make that effort without the methodological perspective provided in economics-as-exchange, or catallactics. The maximizer of social welfare functions could never have written such a book, and, indeed, even today the maximizer of such functions cannot understand what the book is all about.

I have identified the first element or aspect of the inclusive public-choice perspective as the catallactics approach to economics, the economics-as-exchange paradigm. I referred to nineteenth-century economists who urged the catallactics framework for emphasis. I should be remiss here if I should fail to mention that, in my personal case, the acceptance of the catallaxy framework for economic theory emerged not from inquiry into economic methodology directly but rather from the constitutional public-choice perspective that I got from Knut Wicksell. I have often remarked that Wicksell is the primary precursor of modern public-choice theory. Wicksell warned, as early as 1896, against the presumption that we, as economists, give advice to the benevolent despot, to the entity that would, indeed, try to maximize a social welfare function. Wicksell counselled that, if reform in economic policy is desired, we must look to the rules through which economic policy decisions get made, look to the constitution itself. This "politics-as-complex-exchange" notion of Wicksell was the stimulus for me to look more closely into the methodological presuppositions of economics itself, presuppositions that I had really not questioned independently.

Homo Economicus

The second element embodied in the inclusive public-choice perspective that I identified at the beginning of this essay is the behavioral postulate familiarly known as that of *homo economicus*. Individuals are modeled as behaving so as to maximize utilities subject to the constraints they face, and, if the analysis is to be made at all operational, specific arguments must be placed in the utility functions. Individuals must be modeled as seeking to further their own self-interest, narrowly defined in terms of measured net wealth positions, as predicted or expected.

This behavioral postulate is, of course, part and parcel of the intellectual heritage of economic theory, and it has indeed served economists well. It stems from the original contributions of the classical economists themselves, whose great discovery was that individuals acting in pursuit of their own interests may unintentionally generate results that serve the overall "social" interest, given the appropriate framework of laws and institutions. Growing out of these eighteenth-century roots has been the reliance of economists and economics on the *homo economicus* postulate to analyze the behavior of persons who participate variously in markets, and through this, to analyze the workings of market institutions themselves.

No comparable postulate was extended to the behavior of persons in their political or public-choice roles or capacities, either as participants in voting processes or as agents acting for the body politic. There was no such postulate stemming from the classical economists or from their successors. There was no "economic theory of politics" derived from individual choice behavior.

We might, in retrospect, have expected such a theory to have been developed by economists, as a more or less obvious extension of their *homo economicus* postulate from market to collective institutional settings. Once economists turned their attention to politics, they should, or so it now seems, have modeled public choosers as utility maximizers. Why did they not do so? Perhaps the failure of the classical economists, as well as that of their nineteenth-century successors, to take this step might be "excused" by their implicit presumption that collective activities were basically unproductive and that the role of the state was limited largely to what has been called its minimal or protective functions. These economists simply could not conceive that much "good" or "goods" could be generated by collective or governmental action.

But why did their twentieth-century descendants fail similarly, despite some suggestive models as advanced by Wicksell and the Italian public finance scholars in the waning years of the nineteenth century? My own interpretation of the modern failure is that twentieth-century economists had been converted to the maximization-scarcity-allocation-efficiency paradigm, a paradigm that is essentially at variance with that which classical economics embodies, and which draws attention away from individual behavior in exchange contract and toward some presumably objectifiable allocation norm that remains conceptually independent of individual choices. Economic theory, by the third decade of this century, had shifted to a discipline of applied mathematics, not catallaxy. Even markets came to be viewed as "computing devices" and "mechanisms" that may or may not secure idealized allocative results. Markets were not, at base, viewed as exchange institutions, out of which results emerge from complex exchange interaction. Only in this modern paradigm of economic theory could the total absurdity of the idealized socialist structures of Lange-Lerner have been taken at all seriously, as indeed it was and sadly still is, by many practicing economists. We may well ask: Why did economists not stop to ask the questions about why socialist managers would behave according to the idealized rules?

Or, to bring the discussions somewhat further forward in time, why did the economists of the thirties, forties, fifties, and into the sixties take the Keynesian theory of policy seriously? Why did they fail to see the elementary point that elected politicians will seek any excuse to create budget deficits? It all seems so simple in retrospect, but we should not underestimate the difficulties, indeed the moral costs, that are involved in a genuine shift in paradigm, in the very way that we look at the world about us, whether this be economists looking at politics or any other group. It was not easy for economists before the sixties to think of public choosers as utility maximizers in other than some tautological sense. In part, the intellectual blockage here may have stemmed from a failure of those who did advance self-interest models to incorporate the politics-as-exchange paradigm in their own thinking. If politics is viewed only as a potentially coercive relationship among persons, at all levels of conceptualization, then the economist must be either courageous or callous who would model public choosers (whether voters or agents) as net wealth maximizers. Few want to reap the scorn that Machiavelli has received through the ages. Such a world of politics is not at all a pretty place. And analysis based on such a model and advanced as "truth" becomes highly noxious. The very unpleasantness of these models of politics may explain the neglect of what now appear to be clear precursors of this element in the public-choice perspective. Some of the early Italians, notably Pareto, who were themselves perhaps influenced importantly by Machiavelli, seem to have had little or no impact on the thinking of modern social scientists about political process. (Nor, from the middle of this century, has Schumpeter.)

It is only when the *homo economicus* postulate about human behavior is *combined* with the politics-as-exchange paradigm that an "economic theory of politics" emerges from despair. Conceptually, such a combination makes it possible to generate analysis that is in some respects comparable to that of the classical economists. When persons are modeled as self-interested in politics, as in other aspects of their behavior, the constitutional challenge becomes one of constructing and designing framework institutions or rules that will, to the maximum extent possible, limit the exercise of such interest in exploitative ways and direct such interest to furtherance of the general interest. It is not surprising, therefore, to discover the roots of a public-choice perspective that contains both elements in the writings of the American Founders, and most notably in James Madison's contributions to *The Federalist Papers.*

In a very real sense, and with no false modesty, I look on *The Calculus of Consent* as the first contribution in modern public-choice theory that combined and balanced the two critical elements or aspects of the inclusive perspective. And this combination might well not have occurred but for the somewhat differing weights that Gordon Tullock and I brought to our joint venture in that book. I think it is accurate to say that my own emphasis was on modeling politics-as-exchange, under the acknowledged major influence of Knut Wicksell's great work in public finance. By comparison (and interestingly because he was not initially trained as an economist), Tullock's emphasis (stemming from his own experience in and his reflections about the bureaucracy) was on modeling all public choosers (voters, politicians, bureaucrats) in strict self-interest terms. There was a tension present as we worked through the analysis of that book, but a tension that has indeed served us well over the two decades since initial publication.

A Summary Classification

In the sixties and seventies, varying contributions have represented differing weighted combinations of the two central elements in the inclusive public-choice perspective. Works on the theory of bureaucracy and bureaucratic behavior have been weighted toward the *economicus* element, whereas works on constitutional analysis have been more derivative from the politics-as-exchange paradigm. By way of summarizing the discussion, it may be helpful to present a classification of selected items, both classic and modern, in terms of the relative weights assigned the two elements or components in the perspective. I should stress that the classification in the diagram is based on my own subjective estimates. Indeed, readers are invited to make their own classification, and to add additional contributions as desired. The horizontal scale measures the mix between the two elements. Works that emphasize the *homo economicus* postulate lie toward the left-hand pole, while works that emphasize the politics-as-exchange model lie toward the right-hand pole.

Homo Economicus _____ *Politics-as-Exchange*

Hobbes, *Leviathan* (1651)

Madison, *The Federalist
Papers* (1787–1789)

Wicksell,
*Finanztheoretische
Untersuchungen*
(1896)

Schumpeter, *Capitalism,
Socialism and Democracy* (1942)

Downs, *Economic Theory
of Democracy* (1957)

Buchanan-Tullock,
Calculus of Consent (1962)

Tullock, *Politics
of Bureaucracy* (1965)

Rawls, *Theory
of Justice* (1971)

Niskanen, *Bureaucracy and
Representative Government* (1972)

Tullock, *Social Dilemma*
(1975)

Buchanan, *Limits of
Liberty* (1975)

Brennan-Buchanan,
Power to Tax (1980)

Brennan-Buchanan,
Reason of Rules (1985)

3. THE ETHICS OF CONSTITUTIONAL ORDER

EARLY in my own career as a political economist, Robert Dahl and Charles Lindblom published a challenging book entitled *Politics, Economics, and Welfare* (1953). One of the central themes or arguments of the book was that we, as individual citizens, do not make choices among the grand organizational alternatives; we do not choose between "capitalism" and "socialism." We choose, instead, among the pragmatically defined and highly particularized policy alternatives as these are indirectly presented to us through the political process. And we make our choices on the basis of that combination of ignorance, ideology, and interest that best describes our psychological state.

I distinctly recall that I was somehow quite disturbed by this Dahl-Lindblom argument, but that I could not quite work out for myself a fully satisfactory response or counter argument. Perhaps now, nearly four decades later, I can make such an effort.

First, let me translate the problem into terminology that is more familiar to me, and also more general. Let me refer to the whole constitutional order, that is, the structure of legal-political rules, within which we act both in our private and our public capacities. The Dahl-Lindblom thesis is that we do not consciously choose this structure. Empirically, they seem to be correct. We go about making our ordinary choices, which involve complex interactions with other persons and groups, within a framework or a structure of rules that we simply take as a part of our environment, a part of the state of nature, so to speak. This descriptive characterization applies equally to ordinary socio-economic and to political interaction.

If, however, we do not consciously choose, or even think about choosing, among structures of rules, that is, among alternative constitutional orders, how can we be responsible for the regimes under which we live? And if we are not responsible for the ultimate choice among constitutional alternatives and could not, in fact, choose among them, is it not then meaningless to talk about constitutional change or constitutional reform?

The implication seems clear. We must, willy nilly, acquiesce in the regime under which we live, and simply do our best to behave rationally as we confront the pragmatically generated choices that emerge. Something seems wrong with this argument. For most of the time, and for most practical purposes, it is perhaps best that we accept the existing constitutional order as a "relatively absolute absolute" (about which I have more to say in Chapter 5). But such acceptance is not equivalent to a denial that change is possible, even for the single person who thinks about, analyzes, evaluates, and proposes alternative structures. I want to suggest here that each one of us, as a citizen, has an ethical obligation to enter directly and/or indirectly into an ongoing and continuing constitutional dialogue that is distinct from but parallel to the patterns of ordinary activity carried on within those rules that define the existing regime.

Let me illustrate the problem here by reference to a poker game example that will be familiar to those who have ever had any exposure to my own attempts to present the elements of constitutional political economy. In any observed and ongoing poker game, individuals, as players, abide by the rules that exist and that define the game itself. Players adopt this or that strategy in attempts to win within the existing rules. At the same time, however, the same persons may evaluate the rules themselves, and they may enter into side discussions about possible changes in the rules so as to make for a "better" game. If, as a result of such discussion, agreement is reached, then rules are changed and the regime shifts. A new constitution emerges.

This poker example helps me to make two elementary but highly important points. First, the example facilitates the distinction between the choice of strategies within the existing set of rules and the choice among alternative sets of rules, or, more generally, between in-constitutional and constitutional choice. Secondly, the examples allow us to see that an individual, as player, may behave responsibly and rationally in choosing and implementing strategies, within the rules that define the game, without necessarily concerning himself or herself about changes in the rules themselves. That is to say, the individual player may, but need not, enter into the dialogue and discussion about changes in the rules. To remain a player in the game, the choice among strategies of play is necessary, but participation in the potential choice among sets of rules is not necessary. The first of these two points has been elaborated at length in the modern analyses; the second point has not been fully examined, and it provides the focus of attention here.

Let me remain within the more familiar realm of discussion about the first point in order to summarize the now-standard argument. The distinction between the levels of choice, between post-constitutional, or within-rules, choice and choice among rules, has proved helpful in allowing a bridge to be constructed between rational choice behavior by the individual and the emergence of agreement on something that might be called the "general interest." If persons are unable to identify their own narrowly defined interests, due to the presence of some sufficiently thick veil of ignorance or uncertainty, they will choose among alternatives in accordance with some generalizable criteria such as fairness. In this setting of constitutional choice, therefore, no need for an explicit ethical norm seems to arise.

The poker-game, veil-of-uncertainty model has proved helpful in introducing the setting for constitutional choice, and it is a model that I have often used. But the model is highly misleading in respects relevant for my purposes here. If we are considering games with effectively large numbers of participants, there may exist little or no incentive for any single player to participate actively in any serious evaluation of the rules. Each player will, of course, have an incentive to maximize his or her own payoffs within whatever set of rules that exist, and each player may also have an interest in the presence of rules that satisfy generalizable criteria when that player does not know what his or her own position will be. But having the latter interest is not equivalent to having an interest-based incentive to act unless the individual expects that his own action will influence the outcome of the collective selection among alternatives. This point will be familiar to those who recognize the elementary public-choice logic, and especially in application to the theory of rational voter abstention and rational voter ignorance. In a large-number setting, the individual player may not consider himself or herself influential in controlling the ultimate selection among sets of rules; hence, the fully rational player may well refrain from participating in the choice among regimes.

The poker-game analogy is misleading in a second respect, and especially by extension to politics. A poker game is voluntary; hence, rules must, at least in some sense, be agreed to by all players because those who are dissatisfied may withdraw from play altogether. In this context, the large-number setting may not be so problematic as it seems, since each player retains a low-cost exit option. But there is no such exit possible in national political regimes. The political game is compulsory, and we all must play. Individually, therefore, we cannot exercise even residual influence over the rules through an effective exit option. The conclusion is clear: if the individual cannot ultimately influence the choice among regimes, it is not rational to participate actively in any discussion of constitutional change or to become informed about constitutional alternatives.

The argument suggests that becoming informed about, and participating in the discussion of, constitutional rules must reflect the presence of some ethical precept that transcends rational interest for the individual. The individual who acts on such a precept behaves "as if" his or her own influence on the ultimate selection among regimes is more than that which a rational choice calculus would imply. Behavior in accordance with such a precept embodies an ethical responsibility for the choice among regimes.

Note that this ethic of constitutional citizenship is not directly comparable to ethical behavior in interaction with other persons within the constraints imposed by the rules of an existing regime. An individual may be fully responsible, in the standard ethical sense, and yet fail to meet the ethical requirement of constitutional citizenship. The individual may be truthful, honest, mutually respectful, and tolerant in all dealings with others; yet, at the same time, the same individual may not bother at all with the maintenance and improvement of constitutional structure.

On many occasions I have referred to what I have called a loss of constitutional wisdom, and especially as observed over the decades of this century. My argument here suggests that this loss of understanding and loss of interest in political structure may reflect the straightforward working out of rationally based individual self-interest, accompanied by an erosion of the ethical principle of constitutional responsibility. To the extent that we, as individuals, do not act "as if" we do, individually, choose among the grand alternatives, then the constitutional regime that we inherit must be vulnerable both to nonprincipled exploitation and to the natural erosion of historical change.

The result is precisely what we seem to have observed over recent decades. The vision of constitutional order that informed the thinking of James Madison and his peers among the Founders was carried forward for more than a century of our national history. This vision embodies both an understanding of the principles of constitutional order and recognition that the individual, as citizen, must accept the ethical responsibility of full and informed participation in a continuing constitutional convention.

The Madisonion vision, with its embodied ethic of constitutional citizenship, is difficult to recapture once it is lost from the public consciousness. The simple, yet subtle, distinction between strategic choices within rules and constitutional choices among sets of rules, the distinction that was illustrated in the poker-game example introduced earlier, must inform all thinking about policy alternatives. The individual, as citizen, cannot restrict his or her attention to policy options within rules; the individual cannot simply reflect on the alternatives that emerge under the operation of a collective decision rule, say, majority voting in a legislature. Choice cannot be limited to a determination of that which is "best," either in terms of the individual's own interests or in terms of the individual's own version of some general interest. Constitutional citizenship requires that the individual also seek to determine the possible consistency between a preferred policy option and a preferred constitutional structure. (This point may be illustrated by a personal-choice example. An individual may prefer a dish of ice cream, but eating a dish of ice cream may not be consistent with the furtherance of the rules dictated by a self-imposed diet plan, an eating constitution.)

Much of what we have observed in modern politics is best described as action taken without understanding or even consideration of the rules that define the constitutional order. I have referred to this politics as "constitutional anarchy," by which I mean a politics that is almost exclusively dominated by and derivative from the strategic choices made by competing interests in disregard of the effects on political structure. This politics has come to its current position because we, as citizens, have failed to discharge our ethical obligations. We have behaved as if the very structure of our social order, our constitution defined in the broadest sense, will remain invariant or will, somehow, evolve satisfactorily over time without our active participation.

Simple observation of the behavior of our political and judicial agents should indicate that such a faith is totally without foundation. We may, of course, continue to default on the ethical obligation of constitutional citizenship. If we do so, however, we leave unchecked the emerging tyranny of the nonconstrained state, a tyranny that can be dislodged only with revolution. Neither such tyranny nor its consequent revolution is necessary if we, as individuals, can recover, even in part, the ethical principle upon which our constitutional order is established.

We must attend to the rules that constrain our rulers, and we must do so even if such attention may not seem to be a part of a rational-choice calculus. The amorality of acquiescence generates despair and longing; the morality of constitutional understanding embodies hope as a necessary complement.

4. THE RELATIVELY ABSOLUTE ABSOLUTES

Introduction

WHEN I was invited to give the lecture on which this essay is based, I indicated my provisional acceptance on the condition that I be allowed to talk on the topic "The Relatively Absolute Absolutes." I specified this topic for two reasons. First, I am tired of lecturing here, there, and elsewhere on the deficit, tax reform, welfare state, public choice—all topics of some interest to potential audiences and all relevant to some parts of my past work—because these topics do not challenge my deeper current interests. Secondly, I wanted, by announcing a title, to precommit myself and thereby impose a discipline that would force me to write out a lecture on a subject of major importance and one that I have put off for far too long. Further, I have long planned to write a small book on the "relatively absolute absolutes." I hoped that the lecture and this essay, in their preparation and presentation, would at least give me the required introductory shove toward completion.

These are my private, personal reasons for selecting a topic that might seem esoteric and meaningless. I can only hope that I can convey in the following discussion some of the importance and relevance of the relatively absolute absolutes, both in organizing and maintaining a coherent intellectual and moral stance in some highly personalized sense and in providing a practically useful foundation from which to advance persuasive normative judgments on socioeconomic-political alternatives.

I shall mention only three more points by way of preface.

First, I hope I can disturb the complacency of practicing, working economists who never stop to think seriously about either epistemological or normative foundations of their discipline. Secondly, the generalized adherence to the principle of the relatively absolute absolutes is a stance that embodies tolerance on the one hand and continuing tension on the other. It avoids the coziness of both the relativist and the absolutist at the cost of taking on attributes of Janus, attributes of a necessary duality in outlook. Finally, let me emphasize that the principle of the relatively absolute absolutes is not in any sense my own invention. It shows up in many disciplines and in the works of many scholars, often in precisely the same terminology. For my own part, the emphasis derives directly from Frank Knight, who restates the principle in almost every one of his philosophical essays, as well as from Henry Simons, Knight's colleague at the University of Chicago during my salad days at that institution.[1]

Plan for a Book

If and when I write my little book on the relatively absolute absolutes, I propose to develop the argument in a series of separate applications, several of which are familiar. I want to develop applications in economic theory, in psychology, in politics, in epistemology, in law, in sports, in war, in language, in morals, in political philosophy, and perhaps even other disciplines. Through the presentation of these applications, I want to suggest that most of economists do, indeed, accept the principle of the relatively absolute absolutes, even if we do not explicitly realize just what the principle is; that is, even if we do not, in this sense, know what we are doing.

---

1. See, in particular, the essays in Frank H. Knight, *Freedom and Reform* (Indianapolis: Liberty Press, 1982). Also, see Henry Simons, *Economic Policy for a Free Society* (Chicago: University of Chicago Press, 1948).

I shall allocate the limited space in this essay as follows: I shall first introduce an application of the relatively absolute absolutes that is familiar to all economists, although seldom recognized in this particular terminology. Following that, I shall move somewhat beyond orthodox economics into the borderlines with psychology. I shall then introduce an application from politics, one that is again familiar and one that I have long emphasized in my own work, but an application that, again, is not normally discussed under the relatively absolute absolutes rubric. The discussion of these economic, psychological, and political applications can be considered introductory to the central part of the essay, which extends the analysis to moral-ethical discourse. In a sense, the main part of the essay can be interpreted, at least indirectly, as my own response to, or review of, Allan Bloom's best-selling book, *The Closing of the American Mind* (1987), that has been getting so much recent attention.

Marshallian Time: The Long View and the Short

One of Alfred Marshall's central contributions to basic economic theory was his introduction and use of time in analyzing the choices of economic agents, and particularly in the choices made by decision makers for business firms. By heroic and indeed arbitrary abstraction, Marshall imposed a temporal order on the complex environment within which firms act. The process of production involves the organization of costly inputs in the generation of outputs. For some purposes, it is useful to model this process as continuous and simultaneous, without reference to time. But, for Marshall, the timeless model offered little assistance toward an understanding of decision making. He recognized that inputs differ in their specificity, and that contractual obligations embody a time dimension. He proceeded to classify inputs into logically distinguishable and highly stylized categories defined by the time dimension of the choices faced by the firm's agent.

In its simplest formulation, and all that is relevant for my purposes, Marshall distinguished between those inputs that are variable within a short-run period of decision and those inputs that are fixed for decision prospects within such a period. The distinct time periods, the short run and the long run, are themselves defined with reference to input variability, rather than directly in terms of calendar time. The short-period planning decision involves a consideration of alternative rates of output achievable within the limits of variability of the first set of inputs constrained by the fixity of the second set. By contrast, the long-period planning decision involves consideration of alternative rates of output achievable by varying all of the input units as these are optimally adjusted one to another.

This summary sketch of a chapter in elementary price theory illustrates the principle of the relatively absolute absolutes, even if this terminology remains foreign to economic theorists. To demonstrate the meaning of the principle in this application, consider again the short-period planning decision that must be made by the agent for the producing firm. This decision involves the selection of some preferred rate of output, and, in consequence, rates of purchase, hire, or lease of all variable inputs, with the characteristics of the fixed inputs taken as constraints beyond the range of short-period choice. Compare this decision with that which emerges from long-period planning. In the latter, the agent considers alternative levels of fixed input utilization.

For the short-period planning problem, the agent takes the fixed input (the size of physical plant) as an absolute, as a given, a parameter that is not subject to choice within the limits of the relevant planning horizon. At a different level of consciousness, however, the same agent fully recognizes that the fixed inputs are also variable; these inputs shift from the constraint set to the set of objects from which choice becomes possible. It is in this sense that it seems appropriate, and useful, to refer to the fixed inputs as "relatively absolute absolutes" for short-period choice, subject only to variation at a level of consciousness or decision that is conceptually separate from that which defines short-period planning.

Note that the differentiation here is not itself made along a time dimension. The short-period and the long-period planning processes may occur simultaneously. The differentiation lies, instead, in the number of variables that are allowed within the relevant choice-set relative to the number of variables that are relegated to the set of constraints.

Individual Choice within Constraints

In the familiar Marshallian setting, there is some initial starting point when all of the relevant variables are within the choice set. The principle of the relatively absolute absolutes emerges only in choice settings that occur after the initial one. If we extend the analysis to the individual, there is nothing analogous to the creation, *ab initio*, of an institution, as such. An individual does not create himself from nothing. There is no identifiable moment when a person confronts *tabula rasa*, a situation when all of the potential constraints are variables subject to choice. A person's life is an unfolding narrative in which choices are continuously confronted, choices that may determine both subsequent constraints and subsequent preferences. At any moment, an individual finds himself or herself in a setting fully analogous to the agent for the Marshallian firm. The individual must reckon on the temporal adaptability of the potential choice variables, and norms for rational choice require that some variables be treated analogously to fixed inputs in the Marshallian model, that is, as relatively absolute absolutes for the purpose of making short-period choices.

In any choice environment, an individual confronts genuine absolutes, relatively absolute absolutes, and alternatives from which choice may be made. Constraints summarized as genuine absolutes are those described by natural limits, temporal and physical; these are not my concern here. These aside, however, there are relatively absolute absolutes that serve as constraints or boundaries on short-period planning options.

Let us say for the moment that we are professional economists. It remains within the realm of the possible that we could change our profession, and with years of training become physicians or physicists. For most of us, however, it would be rational to take our profession as a given, as a relatively absolute absolute, as a constraint within which relevant choices as to career, work effort, and life-style are made. Within limits, the same argument may, of course, be extended to other characteristics of any person's choice setting. A professional relocation to another employing institution is within the possible, but, for many of us, it may be rational to accept the employment status quo as a constraint, as a relatively absolute absolute, while, at a different level of conscious consideration, we review alternative opportunities. It seems clear that we can extend the same argument to any durable good or service that enters into any consumption or production stream. Durability becomes a reasonably good surrogate for the classification of characteristics into variables and constraints.

Preferences as Constraints

In the two choice settings disclosed, the implicit presumption has been that individual preferences over the relevant choice alternatives are not themselves among the objects for choice. The individual, whether as agent for the firm or for himself, confronts a set of alternatives that is exogenous. If we remain within these standard choice settings, the relatively absolute absolute, as a notion, would be little more than a fancy label for familiar aspects of the general choice problem.

The relatively absolute absolute becomes important as well as useful, however, if we move beyond the choice settings of standard economics, and particularly as we recognize that persons do not approach all choices with a fixed preference ordering over all alternatives. Once we recognize that preferences change and, further, that preferences can be changed by deliberate choice; the temporal differentiation originating from the physical characteristics of the choice options must be replaced by differentiation that is deliberately produced by choice itself.

We may think of a person who chooses to impose upon his or her own choices an artificial preference function, who explicitly adopts rules or norms for choosing among options that exclude some otherwise available options from the choice set, who chooses among options in such fashion as to insure that there will be directional bias in choice patterns actually implemented. Personal examples abound. A person really prefers the calorie-laden dessert, but also wants to maintain or achieve a desirable weight. The "higher" preference, losing weight, constrains the preference for sweets.

The example suggests that an individual may exercise a rational choice among a set of choice alternatives that is, at least in part, determined by his or her own choice exercised at a different level of consciousness. The rule against eating dessert is self-imposed, and is recognized as such. But, for making the cafeteria selections, this precommitment is taken as a relatively absolute absolute. The revealed preference against sweets may reflect a prior preference for preferences, about which the chooser remains fully aware.

It is useful to introduce the term "constitutional" in its most inclusive and general sense here to refer to deliberately chosen constraints on choice alternatives. In the example here, the individual chooses within a set of previously and separately selected precommitments, or rules, which describe a personal constitution for that individual's choice behavior. The point to be emphasized is that the two levels of choice are distinct and that constitutional choice is necessarily more comprehensive than in-constitutional choice.

The Political Constitution

We can move beyond economics while remaining in familiar territory if we shift attention from the personal to the political constitution. In constitutional democracy, and in the United States in particular, it is recognized that ordinary politics takes place within the constraints defined by the set of rules defined as the constitution. The very purpose of these rules is to constrain ordinary political choices. And these ordinary choices take existing constitutional rules as relatively absolute absolutes. As they participate variously in ordinary politics—as voters, aspiring politicians, elected politicians, and bureaucrats—individuals operate within the existing rules of the political game. At the same time, however, individuals recognize that these rules, themselves, at some differing and more comprehensive level of choice, are subject to evaluation, modification, and change. The constitutional rules are not absolutes to be put beyond the pale of rational consideration. But neither are these rules comparable with ordinary politics, which are dominated by current and possibly fleeting dictates of expediency.

Political dialogue and discussion proceed simultaneously at two levels, the in-constitutional and the constitutional. Precisely because constitutional rules are not absolute, they, too, are subject for evaluation and debate. At the same time, and conversely, precisely because they are not subject to change within the decision-making structure of ordinary politics, they can, and do, act to constrain this politics within limits determined by the rules that exist.

We are, as United States citizens, fortunate in that our political structure embodies a much more evident conceptual distinction between the set of constraining rules and the choice-making of politics within that set of rules. Parliamentary democracies, which do not embody such clarity in this distinction, generate confusion, for citizen and scholar alike. Discussion proceeds as if parliamentary majorities operate totally nonconstrained by constitutional rules, while at the same time, some prior commitment to rules for continuing open franchises, along with periodic elections, seems to be presumed in existence. That is to say, politics in parliamentary democracies also proceeds within a set of relatively absolute absolutes, even if these are not explicitly recognized in any formal sense.

Rules for Games

In shifting discussion from personal to political constitutions, we have effected a categorical transformation from private to public choice. The applications from economics suggest the usefulness of modeling strictly private choices in such a manner that decisions made at one level constrain choices at other levels. As we focus on individual choice behavior in interaction with other persons, in a political or social "game," there emerges a new, and conceptually distinct, basis for constitutional precommitment. The individual participant need not, in such a setting, consider it to be useful to impose constraining rules on *his or her own choice behavior.* At the same time, however, since the individual is only one participant in the collective choosing process, and since his own choice need not correspond with that which the collective decision-rule will generate, rational considerations may dictate support for constitutional constraints or limits on the range and scope of collective decisions. In this sense, the individual chooses not to precommit his own choice behavior but rather to constrain the choice behavior of *others than himself,* who might prove dominant in the decision process.

In terms of game theory here, the individual rationally agrees to play by the rules, and to accept these rules as relatively absolute absolutes, not necessarily to constrain his own actions but rather to limit the actions of others than himself. There are two rather than one possible sets of constraining rules once we move into social interaction, once we consider games between and among separate decision-making units. The first set of rules is that which defines the game itself, those rules that constrain the actions of individual players and which are applicable to all players. These are, in a sense, public rules. There may be, but need not be, a different set of constraining rules, through which a single player may, independently of other players, constrain his own choices as he plays the game in accordance with the public rules. This second set of possible constraints may be called private rules; these need not constrain all players, and such rules need not be comparable over all players.

The second set of rules, private rules, are those of the personal constitution discussed earlier. But, in social interaction, we often refer to these rules as individualized strategies, rules that dictate to a player how choices will be made over a whole sequence of plays of a game. In sports, reference is often made to a team's or a player's game plan, which is to be distinguished both from the rules of the game itself and from the tactics of play within these rules. But the game plan, as such, also constrains the choices within the tactical setting. And, as the player attempts to follow the game plan, he is behaving as if this plan is relatively absolute absolute.

The same logical structure is often applied to discussion of wars or conflict between opposing parties or groups. The common distinction is between strategy and tactics. And, especially in earlier centuries, even wars were conducted within implicit rules for the game itself. This aside, however, military strategy for a campaign describes a set of constraining rules within which tactical choices are to be made. The strategy is treated as being relatively absolute absolute when tactical decisions are made, while at the same time, the commander considers shifting the strategy itself.

Epistemology

What I have covered to this point will have seemed repetitious and redundant to those who are at all acquainted with my published writings of recent vintage. I have deliberately gone over familiar ground in preparation for the important applications of the principle of the relatively absolute absolutes, at least from my own perspective. Let me first consider epistemology, a branch of inquiry that occupies so many of the good minds of this and other times. How do we know anything once we recognize that all knowledge must, somehow, be filtered through our minds, which, in turn, translate perceptions into ideas? I have never been attracted to go deeply into epistemology; at the same time, I have never felt at a loss before the highly complex set of issues discussed by my learned colleagues. My own ability to withstand temptation in this respect has, I think, its foundations in the relatively absolute absolute.

I am able, armed with this principle, to proceed as if we do indeed possess knowledge, even if at another level of inquiry I can realize that we may not. I can keep in lockstep with the positivist, who accepts the genuine reality of the world to be discovered and literally believes that this reality exists, while at the same time I can express agreement with those antipositivist critics, provided only that the argument be carried on at a separate and distinct level of discourse. The real world exists, as a relatively absolute absolute, and we can get on with our work.

I can take much the same stance toward the whole Popperian enterprise, with its emphasis on the falsifiability of hypotheses and on the provisionality of all truth. Ordinary or everyday science proceeds as if its hard core Lakatosian program embodies a set of relatively absolute absolutes. Scientists can work within this methodological framework without being frustrated by the deeper epistemological issues around the edges. We may, on occasion, walk on ice as if it were solid ground, even if we recognize that to do so requires that certain conditions of temperature, time, and place be met.

Value Relativism

I now turn to the alleged relativism of all values. For well over a century, or with philosophers indeed since David Hume, we have lived with the collapse of certitude previously offered by the dogmas of religion and reason. Blueprints outlining either the precepts of behavior for the "good man" or the principles of the "good society" are not to be found on tablets left on mountaintops or in communion with the spirits of ancient Greeks. Modern human beings seem to be trapped in the dilemma imposed by the disappearances of moral-ethical absolutes. Where does the individual turn when he or she is unable to counter Dostovoesky's "all is permitted" or Cole Porter's "anything goes"? If we are, ourselves, the ultimate source of evaluation, how can disparate value norms be ordered, either within the psyche of an individual or as advanced by separate persons?

It is precisely when such questions as these are posed that resort to the principle of the relatively absolute absolutes is most useful. This principle combines the desired ordering properties of moral-ethical absolutism with the equally esteemed properties of intellectual integrity. It offers us a philosophical standing place between the two equally unacceptable extremes, between the pretension and arrogance of the moral absolutist on the one hand, and the total abnegation of judgmental capacity on the other.

The evocation and utilization of the principle of the relatively absolute absolutes depends critically on our ability and willingness both to choose among constraints and to act within the constraints that are chosen. In the absence of self-imposed constraints, we are simple human animals. And a measure of our advance from this animal state is provided by the distance that separates us from the internally anarchistic psychological benchmark defined by the total absence of self-imposed rules.

As Frank Knight emphasized, a human being is a rule-following animal. We live in accordance with a set of moral-ethical rules or norms for behavior, a set that we take, consciously or unconsciously, to be relatively absolute absolutes. We do not, and should not, treat these norms for our behavior as having been revealed to us by god or by reason. Nor should we treat these norms as sacrosanct merely because they exist as a product of a cultural evolutionary process that we may not fully understand. These personal norms are appropriate objects for critical inquiry and discussion, which may proceed at one level of our consciousness while we continue to choose and to act by the very dictates of these norms in our behavior as ordinary persons. We can, upon reflection, evaluate, criticize, and ultimately change the rules that describe "the constitution of our values." But it is vitally important to recognize the categorical distinction between this change in the moral constitution of ourselves and ordinary changes in such matters as diet, dress, recreational activity, and sexual partners.

Political Philosophy

My suggestion that the principle of the relatively absolute absolutes offers a philosophical standing place between the extremes of moral relativism and moral absolutism may be readily accepted in application to the realm of personal values that determine private rules. But I have not, to this point, demonstrated the applicability of the principle to public rules, to the commonality of values among persons, or, in more general terms, to political philosophy.

First of all, it is necessary to define the origin from which any discussion is to proceed. It is worth emphasizing that this origin is the individual who is identified in physical and temporal dimensions. The individual finds himself or herself located in time and place, with a genetic and cultural history, which includes participation in interactions with other persons, who are recognized to be reciprocally capable of choosing among constraints and acting within the constraints so chosen, both in their private and public choosing-acting roles.

To the extent that social interaction exhibits predictable patterns of order, there must exist rules or norms for individual behavior that are common over many participants. These shared public rules must, however, be operative in a setting that allows separate individuals to hold widely divergent constitutions of personal, private values in the sense discussed above. A central task of political philosophy is to derive principles of social order that will reconcile divergent private value structures and the minimally required public rules without which productive interaction among persons is impossible.[2] These public rules may be formal, as embodied in law and legal institutions, or they may be informal, as reflected in prevailing conventions. To the individual, these public rules exist; they define an aspect of the environment within which the individual chooses and acts. These rules exist as a precondition for participation in the "game" of social order. And the individual, any individual, must accept these public rules as relatively absolute absolutes. The fact that the individual may not have participated, actually and effectively, in the choice process that generated the set of public rules, if indeed such a process did take place, is irrelevant to his or her acceptance. In this respect, public rules are functional absolutes in ongoing social order. But they remain open to evaluation and change; these rules are relative rather than absolute absolutes.

At the appropriate level of inquiry, the individual may participate in an examination of the desirability of the existing set of public rules, an examination that must include comparison with alternative sets. But the process of evaluation here can only take place separately and apart from the continued interaction of all participants within the existing status quo set of rules. Individuals who privately abrogate public rules by violating those in existence, thereby imposing their own preferred rules on others, become, quite literally, outlaws, and deserve treatment as such.

My argument that the status quo set of public rules must be treated as a set of relatively absolute absolutes is not equivalent to assigning this set of rules some superior moral attribute in the relevant long-run or constitutional sense. In a setting where persons'

---

2. See John Gray, "Contractarian Method, Private Property, and the Market Economy" (Jesus College, Oxford, December 1986, Mimeographed).

basic values differ, we should expect that the set of public rules observed to be in existence will be nonoptimal to *everyone,* when evaluated against a given individual's ideal principles for social interaction. At the same time, however, the set of public rules may be optimal in the Pareto sense familiar to welfare economists, there may be no change that could be agreed to by *all* members of the community. Peaceful coexistence requires that we treat as relatively absolute absolutes those institutions or rules of social interaction within which relationships are orderly rather than conflictual. These rules remain only relatively absolute, however, and they are always subject to inquiry, evaluative comparison, and reform, upon agreement among all affected persons and groups.

The central point to be emphasized is that the process of living rationally and efficiently within the public rules that exist must be understood to remain categorically distinct from potential discussion and rationally derived changes in these rules. To revert to the initial Marshallian analogy, the firm may be in long-run disequilibrium with the wrong size of its plant, but it remains rational for it to operate that plant which exists optimally.

I consider it to be the task of economists, as economic scientists, to make rudimentary predictions about the behavior of persons within existing and potential constraints, whether these be imposed physically or artifactually. I have considered it to be the task of economists, as moral and social philosophers, to evaluate alternative sets of constraints, and to seek consensus on changes in the direction of those that most nearly meet the discipline's ultimate normative criteria, which are themselves determined by agreement. I have found, personally, that the principle of the relatively absolute absolutes has been very helpful in sorting my way through the complex intellectual mazes that confront all economists. I hope that, in this very preliminary sketch of what I hope will be a more comprehensive effort, I have been able to suggest to others the productivity of a single simple idea.

5. ON THE WORK ETHIC

JANUARY 3 and 4, 1987, were the Saturday and Sunday of the four seasonal National League playoff games. Like many others, I wanted to watch all four of these football games on television. But, also like many others, perhaps, I felt guilty about spending some ten to fifteen hours over two days sitting in front of a television screen. But there are limits to feelings of guilt, and I was guilt-ridden only until I remembered that, a month or so earlier, I had picked up a half-bushel of black walnuts from a tree in my yard, and these walnuts had not yet been shelled. So I proceeded to get out an old flatiron and put it on my lap with a hammer and a nutpick and two big bowls. And then for ten to fifteen hours, I cracked and shelled black walnuts while I watched those four playoff games. This by-product activity served to assuage my feelings of guilt. I had the sense that I was accomplishing something, and I produced in the process two quarts of black walnuts, shelled, which is no small feat.

It was this personal experience that got me started to think about the work ethic. In the first place, I felt guilty because I was saddled with this old-fashioned work ethic, sometimes called the Puritan ethic. It is a part of my psyche, a part that is probably so deeply embedded in my consciousness that it is immovable by ordinary processes of rational thinking. Shelling the walnuts salved my conscience because it amounted to *doing* something,

47

producing something of value. But I raised the question to myself: Is all this a genetic residue of some primitive premodern ethic, a norm that may have made sense in the setting where subsistence itself was at stake, but a norm that has since lost all *raison d'etre* in our affluent society? Does the work ethic mean anything today, in the late eighties of the twentieth century? Or does the choice between work and leisure, work and idleness, matter not at all? Why not acknowledge that this choice is relevant to each individual who makes it? How can we condemn on any ethical or moral grounds the university graduate or skilled technician who simply chooses to live his life in sloth? Perhaps modern schools have already thrown out the nursery rhymes and folk tales that praise work and condemn indolence. Perhaps I am the one who is out of touch with modern reality. These questions seemed worth a bit of pondering. During the whole week of the great snow in January 1987 I stewed around and bothered my colleagues about it.

There seems to be a gaping hole in formal economic theory here. No one seems to have tried to establish analytical foundations, if there are any, to this old-fashioned work ethic. And taken literally, the implication to be drawn from formal economic theory is that there is no ethical content in the work-leisure choice of an individual. Translated into my personal example, the inference would be that whether or not I shelled those black walnuts affected me and me alone, and hence there were no effects on anybody else in the social order. Formal economic theory seems to tell me this; if so, then something seems to be wrong with formal economic theory. I had to go back to the foundations of the formal analysis to see what had gone wrong, for I remained convinced that the traditional wisdom embodied in the common words "work" and "ethic" was somehow correct. This is not the time or place to explain the logical reasoning I had to go through to convince myself that the work ethic does indeed have meaning. I hope that eventually I can convince some referees and editors of professional economics journals that I have filled a gap in the formal theory. But in a very real sense, this point, like so much else that I have done in my own contributions, is much easier to put across to anyone with a little common sense than it is to the professional economist who already has several sets of mental blinders.

The question, of course, is a very simple one. Why is work good, and why is loafing bad? Let us think about this a little. The answer is at the same time very easy and very difficult. First of all, I want to eliminate the personal feedback aspect of any argument. I do not want to rely on the notion that work is good for you because it instills habits that will be of value. I want to ask why work is good in and of itself and apart from any future effects on the person who chooses to work or to loaf. That is to say the word "good" in the way I want to use it here implies that my choice benefits others in the community, that work is externally evaluated in a positive way, whereas loafing is somehow evaluated negatively. The sticking point in formal economic theory lies in the fact that work is rewarded. When I choose to work, or to shell walnuts, I produce something of value; and my contribution to value is precisely equivalent to the wage-rate, salary, or price that I get for my efforts. This being the case, how can my private decision about whether to work or to loaf affect anyone but myself?

This line of reasoning ignores a fundamental lesson taught to us by Adam Smith in 1776. There are gains from the division of labor, from specialization in production accompanied by exchange or trade. Hence the act of entering into the exchange nexus itself generates benefits to everyone else in the nexus, and the work-leisure choice of an individual always involves just such an act.

Think of a simple example. Jones and Smith are frontier

farmers. They live side by side, but each one of them is totally self-subsistent. Each grows his own potatoes and his own pigs. There is no specialization, no division of labor, and no trade. But each man then realizes that both can gain by entering into a specialization and exchange relationship. Jones begins to specialize in growing potatoes; Smith begins to specialize in growing pigs. Then they swap the potatoes and the pigs. Both are made better off; each can consume both more potatoes and more pigs. Each person has, in choosing to enter this economic arrangement, conferred benefits both on himself and his trading partner.

This is of course an elementary story from the very primer of economics. But we must recognize that every time we choose, individually and privately, to work an additional hour, an additional day, an additional week, we are, in so doing, entering the exchange nexus. We are producing goods that are valued by others, and even though we are paid in full for value produced for others, there remains a residue of value to be shared with others. In loafing, there is no spillover share in the excess value produced. The value in loafing is exclusively internal to the person who does the loafing. The argument suggests that there is ethical content in the work-leisure choice of the individual, that the traditional folk wisdom is indeed correct, that we may legitimately and on the basis of a rational choice calculus deem work to be praiseworthy and loafing to be blameworthy. And this conclusion emerges without maternalistic or meddlesome preferences for any sort or work or consumption pattern the individual may choose to adopt. So long as work adds something of value in exchange, there is a social spillover benefit that is absent in leisure except as is internal to the person who chooses it.

I have laid out the elements of an argument to the effect that each of us will indeed be doing good to others, and for others than ourselves, every time we choose to work rather than to loaf, and even if we receive the full market value of that which we work at or produce. Remember this at those times when you are out there in the great world of economic reality trying to earn a buck. When someone tells you to "stop and smell the flowers," remember that it is you, not him or her, who is doing good.

6. FREE TRADE AND PRODUCER-INTEREST POLITICS

Introduction

CLASSICAL liberals have often disagreed sharply over particular policy issues. I recall heated exchanges between those who advocate return to monetary stability by way of the gold standard and those who advocate some variant of a rule-directed monetary authority. I recall disputes between those who have favored floating rate and fixed rate international monetary arrangements. And at a more philosophical level, the relationship between religion and the economic order has often been a source of difference in attitudes.

The listing of particular issues over which classical liberals have differed and do differ could be extended. But I do not recall any expressed clashes of opinion on the desirability of free trade, whether among persons within nations or among persons of different nations. Free trade is, I suggest, one issue that allows classical liberals to define themselves. The observed fact that those who do understand the simple logic of free trade (which is perhaps as good a definition of economists as any other, even if the definition is grounded in practical understanding rather than technical skill) have not been at all successful in disseminating our message is, of course, discouraging. And often we may despair when we think how little public or general understanding has changed since Adam Smith mounted his attack on mercantilism in 1776. On the other hand, our very *raison d'etre*, as economists in the sense defined above, lies in the continuing need that this logic of free trade be repeated, reiterated, and applied, even to the point of ennui. It is too easy to lose faith in the ultimate ability of ideas to shape events and, in so doing, to shed the moral obligation to carry the message.

I shall take as self-evident, for my purposes here, the welfare economics of free trade, and propose instead to discuss what I shall call the "welfare politics" of free trade (thereby putting my own spin on Paul Samuelson's early and somewhat derisory characterization of public-choice theory). Despite the generalized normative argument that stems from the familiar principles of economics (which classical liberals universally accept), politically imposed restrictions on voluntary exchanges seem pervasive, whether within national economies or between persons and organizations which seek to trade across national boundaries. The utilitarian-efficiency norm, as such, seems to carry relatively little political weight.

In a certain preliminary way, public-choice theory seems to explain much of that which we observe in political reality. The influence of specialized interest or pressure groups, organized by producer classifications, on the institutions of democratic governance generate analytically predictable patterns of restrictions, interferences, and controls over market exchanges. From this elementary public-choice analysis, however, a question emerges about limits. Why is not market restriction even more widespread than we observe it to be?

I want to extend the application of public choice theory beyond the initial stages of explanation. I want to suggest that there may be more vitality in the free trade logic than simplistic interest-group models of democratic process may indicate. My thesis may be stated straightforwardly: The potential gains from restrictions on voluntary exchange are more apparent than real, even to the input owners or producers who seek and secure the particularized benefits of such restrictions. The interests of the unorganized (and presumably unorganizable) consumers, as such, need not be expressly or directly represented. Under plausibly realistic assumptions concerning effective coalition sizes, voting rules, excess burdens, organizing and enforcement costs, and rent-seeking investment, a genuine utility-maximizing calculus may dictate support for *constitutional* prohibition of all market restrictions by most members of the body politic, including those producer interests that might be considered to be potentially identifiable beneficiaries of restrictions. Careful consideration of the inclusive "welfare politics" here suggests that free trade, if examined as and presented as a *constitutional* alternative, may be more viable than it seems in the stylized analysis of interest-group interaction within ordinary politics.

An alternative way of describing the content of my argument is to say that it offers a demonstration of the feasibility of free trade, as an object of constitutional reform, without the requirement that participants in the economy-polity be placed behind some Rawlsian veil of ignorance and/or uncertainty in either an actualized or conceptualized setting for choice. The free trade option, constitutionally considered, may be Pareto-preferred to the restrictionist status quo even when all persons are identified by their roles in producer interest groups, and even when complex compensation schemes are not considered feasible. Participants' constitutional interests may dominate their particular interests, and the convergence of agreement in the former may become the means of overcoming the inherent conflict in the latter. In this setting, the reaching of agreement on the constitutional regime of free trade may be the equivalent of escaping from the n-person analogue to the prisoners' dilemma that a protectionist regime describes.[1]

---

1. For an elaboration of the distinction between constitutional interests and particular interests, see Viktor Vanberg and James Buchanan, "Rational Choice and Moral Order" (CPC, 1987, Mimeographed).

Producer/Sellers as Consumer/Buyers

It will be necessary here for me to introduce some stylized economic theory, but I promise to keep the argument in ordinary language.

Consider an initial setting in which the economy is organized competitively, and there is free trade both within the economy and among organizations within the economy and other economies, separated politically from the first. Assume that each industry is organized along producer lines. The particular economic interests of any producer group, treated as an organized unit, is to secure a protected or monopoly position in the market for the good or service that is produced and marketed. In order to simplify the analysis dramatically, I want to assume that any potential gains from market restriction or protection will be shared among all persons who supply inputs to the industry at the time that the restriction is put in place. Any person in the industry will therefore be made better off by the closing of the market to new producers, domestic or foreign, and by the political enforcement of cartel quotas on production.

Now let us examine the prospect for political action on a proposal for protection or cartelization of a single industry, which we can call Industry 1. By our assumption, all other industries are organized along producer lines, even though they remain internally competitive. Rational choice behavior on the part of all industry groups, other than Industry 1, will dictate opposition to the proposal for restriction on Industry 1. The interests of all members of other industries, in their roles as consumers-buyers of the product of Industry 1, will be damaged by the imposition of restrictions on the single market. Taken one at a time and singly, proposals for restricting entry into or production within markets do not seem politically viable.

This elementary reality of politics will of course be recognized by any producer group that seeks restriction. Each group that initiates action to further restriction in its own market will reckon that a coalition of groups is required here. In order to generate support for restrictions in the market for the good it produces and sells, a single industry group will recognize that it must also support, reciprocally, similar restrictive proposals for other producing groups that it may join in a coalition.

Again let us simplify the analysis by some stylized assumptions. Suppose there are many (n) industry or producer groups in the economy, and these are of roughly equal size in number of persons supplying inputs. Assume further that political decisions are made as if by simple majority voting rules. This implies that, in order for a protectionist or supply-restricting coalition to become politically viable, a minimum winning coalition of slightly more than one-half of the producing groups must be brought into agreement. That is to say, in order to secure the restriction desired on the single producer group's market, there must be comparable restriction extended to one-half of the other markets in the economy.

Consider now the position of a single producer group that becomes a potential member of such a coalition. It expects to secure the monopoly gains that restriction of entry into its own market seems to offer. But it must also expect to incur losses from the similar restrictions that will be imposed on one-half of the other markets in the economy. Rational choice will dictate that the single group will reckon on these losses it must incur as customers in other restricted markets, as an offset to the expected gains from restriction in its own market.

There are interesting implications to be drawn from the elementary analysis. The net gains that any producer group can expect to secure from politicized enforcement of market restrictions are very substantially below those that might be thought to be possible under single-industry isolated restriction. For purposes of numerical illustration, let us postulate that a single producer group, if it could secure isolated restriction on its own market, would secure positive net rents or profits in the amount of $2X$, with an overall loss to consumers generally of $3X$. (In language familiar to economists, the monopoly profits are double the deadweight losses or excess burden.)[2] If, in order to get restriction in its own market, the producer group must join in a coalition with one-half of the other producing groups in the whole economy, and if each group in the coalition acts as if it is in isolation in terms of output restriction, the prospective gains from restriction to the single group are reduced from $2X$ to $X/2$, that is, by three-fourths.[3]

The size of the reduction in the prospective net gain to be secured from market restriction will, of course, depend directly on the size of the coalition of producer groups that must simultaneously secure protection. Any single industry will, ideally, seek to secure restriction in its own market in isolation, as a single-member coalition. As the effective size of the coalition increases, the gains from generalized restriction fall. The simple example discussed above was based in the simple arithmetic of majority governance. But in the complex setting of modern politics, an effective coalition may be made up of less than or more than half of all producer groups.[4]

---

2. This result emerges from the simple model where demand and cost schedules are linear.

3. The example is, of course, highly stylized. It assumes that all producer groups are similar in size, that there are no nonproducers, and that patterns of producers as consumers are similar. More significantly, the particular result emerges only if we assume that enforcement costs prevent the optimal degree of output restriction for members of the restricted coalition of producer groups. Clearly it will be to the interest of each member of the coalition to agree to output restrictions, extended uniformly over all member groups, that are less severe than those that are optimal under isolated single-group market restriction.

4. For one of the few papers that analyzes the efforts of a coalition of producer groups in policy outcomes, see R. H. Bates and W. P. Rogerson, "Agriculture in Development: A Coalition Analysis," *Public Choice* 35, no. 5 (1980): 513–528.

Rent Seeking

To this point, I have assumed that organizational, enforcement, and rent-seeking costs are absent. The effective coalition of producer groups in the economy has been assumed to be able to secure political action enforcing restriction or protection on all of the markets represented in the coalition with no investment at all by coalition members. I now propose to introduce rent seeking, while continuing to ignore organizational and enforcement costs.

Assume, then, that in order to generate political action that will impose enforceable restrictions in the market represented in the coalition, investment must be made in varying forms of persuasion by all potential members of the free coalition. Legislators and bureaucrats must be entertained; advocates must be hired; briefs must be prepared; arguments must be analyzed; rhetoric must be rehearsed; demonstrators must be demonstrated. And each of such activities uses up economically valued resources.

How much will a single producing interest, an industrially organized entity charged with making decisions for the group, be willing to invest in order to insure that the good it produces and sells is artificially limited in supply, thereby generating net rents or profits? Let us return to the stylized numerical illustration that was introduced earlier. Recall that, in the case where the effective minimal coalition includes one-half of the total number of separately organized producer groups, the prospective gains from membership in the restricted or protected coalition are $X/2$, at least in the stylized setting postulated. How much will a single producing interest be willing to invest to insure that it can retain this rent or profit potential?

An answer to this question requires a comparison with the position of a producing interest, already organized, that remains outside the successful protected-restricted coalition. Such a producer group finds itself operating, as a set of producing units, in an open and unrestricted market environment. At the same time, however, this unprotected producing group finds itself faced with the requirement of purchasing goods from the one-half of the economy that is protected at rent or profit maximizing prices. The nonmember of the coalition will suffer a $3X/2$ loss in buyers' or consumers' surplus, by comparison with that surplus which could be enjoyed in an economy where all industries are open to competition.[5]

The difference, therefore, between the economic position of a successful member of the restrictive-protected coalition, measured by $X/2$ in our example here, and the position of an unsuccessful producer group that remains outside the coalition, measured as a minus $3X/2$ in the example, is much larger than the size of the positive gain that might be expected to emerge under successful membership. The difference in our example is $2X$. And it is this difference between the two positions that will offer the motivation for rent-seeking investment. If a producing group makes no rent-seeking investment and simply acquiesces in confrontation with the rent-seeking activity of other groups, it will be damaged. In order to prevent the coercively imposed damage, any group will have some incentive to invest in efforts to become a member of the coalition, to secure political action that will enforce protection on its own market.

It seems evident, and even without the numerical examples here, that rent seeking may more than exhaust the positive rents that are finally attained by those who are successful winners in the protectionist game. As the example suggests, the gain is only $X/2$ if the entrant is successful; this gain is offset by a loss of $3X/2$ if the entrant is unsuccessful. Rent-seeking investment of more than $X/2$

---

5. The algebra is straightforward. A total loss of $3X$ is imposed on consumers generally by each market that is restricted. There are $n/2$ markets so restricted, for a total loss of $3/2 \times n$, which is shared by all n groups. Hence, each group loses $3X/2$ as consumers.

on the part of a single producer group seems highly plausible and even probable.[6]

Suppose, however, that a producer group invests, say X, in securing political support for restrictions on its own market. Suppose further that this group, along with one-half of all other groups, is successful. The desired restriction is secured. Domestic output is restricted; the industry is cartelized; domestic entrants are kept out; foreign entrants are shut off; prices are increased; rents emerge. But note that the investment of X exceeds the net positive rent. The successful producing interest would be better off in a setting where no group seeks protection than it is in the successful coalition of protected industries.

The positive rents are more than dissipated; there is superexhaustion of all gains.[7] The groups that invest in efforts to secure

---

6. Rent-seeking investment may take one form of efforts by groups outside the protected coalition to organize opposition to restrictive political action rather than efforts to join in the coalition either as additional or replacement members. In a seminar presentation at George Mason University in 1986, Gordon Tullock introduced a model in which individuals face choices between joining a logrolling coalition and organizing an opposing coalition.

7. This discussion of overdissipation or superexhaustion is stimulated by discussions with Ron Heiner, who has worked out, both analytically and experimentally, the necessary settings in which such phenomena can occur. See Ron Heiner, "Superexhaustive Rent Seeking" (Brigham Young University, July 1987, Mimeographed).

The early models of rent seeking suggested full dissipation, although later developments have indicated that, under varying structural settings, under-, full-, or over-dissipation can occur. The standard models have, however, incorporated the implicit assumption that some institutional analogue to voluntary withdrawal from the rent-seeking game is present. It is precisely the absence of this feature that characterizes the "game" analyzed here.

For the early models, along with later developments in the theory of rent seeking, see two collections: *Toward a Theory of the Rent Seeking Society*, ed. J. Buchanan, R. Tollison, and G. Tullock (College Station: Texas A & M University Press, 1980), and *The Political Economy of Rent Seeking*, ed. C. Rowley, R. Tollison, and G. Tullock (Boston: Kluwer-Nijhoff, 1988).

restrictions and protection for their own markets will, of course, lose even more than they do by acquiescing in the coerced imposition of damages by the successful restrictions on other markets. Note however that, in this setting, no single producer group, no representative of an industry or market, will have any incentive to act unilaterally to reduce rent-seeking effort. Consider the member of the successful coalition, which has invested X in rent seeking, and which has gained only $X/2$ in positive rents as profits. This group is worse off than it would be in the fully competitive economy. But if such a group should try unilaterally to reduce its rent-seeking outlay, it will quickly find itself among those producer interests whose market remains unprotected, and with a much larger net loss than it experiences under the protective umbrella of the coalition.

The addition of positive organizational costs and enforcement costs does not substantially modify the analysis. These costs of the separately defined producing interests can be added onto the rent-seeking costs in determining the final position of either the successful or the unsuccessful groups. The higher the organizational and enforcement costs the lower will be the anticipated net gains from politically orchestrated restrictions on the relevant markets.

Constitutional Implications

The direction of my argument should be clear. In an economy where the coalition of producer interests required to generate political support for market restrictions is relatively large, the protectionist game may become negative sum, even for those interests that are net "winners." This result becomes increasingly probable as rent-seeking investment is taken into account. Despite the negative-sum attribute, however, no single interest will have an incentive to withdraw from the rent-seeking effort; no interests will unilaterally opt for a removal of the restrictive barriers to its own market.

There is no analogue here to withdrawal from the game, which would, of course, take place if the game was genuinely voluntary. Because the producing interests must remain within the same economy, and must at the same time be consumers of goods from other industries, any and all interests are subject to the exploitation that market restriction makes possible. Hence, withdrawal of effort to secure protection for its own market would amount to a bizarre preference for increased net losses. There is no analogue to the zero-sum benchmark that characterizes genuinely voluntary games here.

Note that the negative-sum attribute of a solution that seems possible here may be relatively difficult to detect. The "winners" in the protectionist-restrictionist game are damaged relative to the position they would be able to secure under generalized competitive conditions extended over the whole economy. But this difference is measured by an opportunity loss of surplus (utility) that does not, and cannot, enter into a standard calculus of interests. In the stylized model analyzed here, input owners-suppliers in the "winning" industries will still be observed to receive payments above those received by input owners in "losing" industries. The "winners" would therefore be reluctant to opt for a change in the rules such that their own returns would be brought into equality with those who are currently "losers" in the protectionist-restrictionist game. Such reluctance can only be overcome by placing an emphasis on the gains in surplus that can be potentially secured by all producing interests from a shift to generalized competitive markets or free trade.

The particular feature of the negative-sum game that makes this shift more readily attainable is the generalization of the negative-sum attribute over all players or participants. In the standard or orthodox welfare economics of trade, the existence of deadweight loss or excess burden insures that any restriction on freedom of voluntary exchange or trade guarantees that the game will be negative sum. The losers from market restrictions always lose more than the gainers gain. Hence, if a system of idealized compensations could be worked out, the gainers could always compensate the losers and a return to free trade would be possible. But, as I suggested earlier, the politics of trade restrictions suggest that this elementary economics cuts relatively little ice in political reality. What the model in this essay aims to show, however, is that the negative-sum attribute need not require a summing of losses and benefits over all players. The model demonstrates, or at least intends to demonstrate, that *all* players may suffer net losses in the protectionist-restrictionist political solution. And, since *all* groups are net losers, by comparison with the positions that could be attained under generalized free trade, it may be in the direct economic interest of each group, taken in isolation and independently, to support a shift in regime toward free trade. There may be no need for the political economist to work out, and for political entrepreneurs to implement, complex compromises, compensations, and the like in order to secure the agreement on the part of the apparent winners. There are "winners" here only in some relative or rank-order sense. These "winners" as well as the losers gain from the removal of all protective-restrictive barriers to freedom of trade. All of the potential compensations are, therefore, internal to the calculus of the separate "players," who are, in our case, the separate producing interests organized over the separate markets of the economy.

As noted earlier, however, no producing group that "enjoys" the politically enforced protection of its own market will find it advantageous, unilaterally, to seek removal of the protective umbrella. The structure of the game dictates that the rules be changed, and the negative-sum attributes, generalized over all participants, suggest that it may be in the economic interests of all players to prefer a shift in the rules. All interests, including those who have enjoyed protection for their own goods markets, will support a rules change, or regime change, that will eliminate all protectionist-restrictionist measures and introduce free trade in *all* markets. That is to say, all groups may agree on genuinely *constitutional* reform in the rules for trade.

Toward a Constitutional Reform Strategy

The central argument of this discussion does not depend critically on the precise results developed either in the analysis or the numerical illustration. The lapse into standard and stylized economic theory was designed to provide a basis for understanding the principle. We know, of course, that economies are not organized into many equal-sized producer groups; we know that nonproducer interests exist, most of which remain unorganized and unrepresented in political decision structures. We also know that modern democratic politics may indeed operate to favor highly concentrated minority interests that are not necessarily combined into logrolled majority coalitions, despite the nominally majoritarian feature of legislative rules. We must also recognize that there remain serious intellectual barriers to the understanding of the elementary logic of free trade. Producer interests in and gains from market restrictions and market protections are readily apparent; consumer interests in and gains from free trade are much less obvious.

At the same time, however, and by way of partial offset, genuine constitutional reform need not require the unanimous agreement that the preceding analysis has suggested to be possible under certain circumstances. There will, presumably, always exist some producing interests that can secure positive net gains from politically enforced cartelization, even when rent-seeking costs are fully taken into account and even when the protected umbrella is widely extended. But, if those who suffer net losses from generalized trade restrictions, both within and without the protected umbrella, make up a sufficiently large share of the total membership in the polity, the few outlying net gainers can be overwhelmed in the qualified majority consensus that may be required to implement constitutional change.

Several elements for a strategy of constitutional reform may be suggested. The analysis has been designed to demonstrate that, at least in some settings, those organized producer interests that seem to secure gains from market restrictions may suffer net losses relative to their positions under a constitutionally enforced regime of genuinely free trade. This result requires that restrictions on voluntary exchange in and entry into markets be relatively widespread and, further, that any organized producer interest might consider the rent potential promised by politically generated interferences in the market for its own good. Those academic and legal advocates who seek to further free trade as a normative ideal should therefore seek first to break down overt discrimination among separate producer interests or commodity categories that might suggest specialized treatment. If politically enforced market restraints are applied to some industries, argument must be mounted to suggest that some internal equivalent to the most-favored-nation clause in international trade should be applied to insure that, in principle, comparable restraints should be extended to all industries. Or, in terms of an even more general philosophical principle, equality of legal treatment can here be interpreted to mean that all producer groups deserve comparable market restraint. Those representatives for organized producer interests who demand differentially discriminatory treatment for their own markets must be called into account. Justificatory argument must be generalized across markets if it is to be deemed acceptable.

In his seminal book *A Theory of Justice* (1971), John Rawls used an idealized contractarian procedure to derive *equal liberty* as the lexically prior principle of justice. Free trade, defined as the freedom of all individuals to enter voluntary exchanges, one with another, is fully consistent with this fundamental principle of equal liberty. Restricted trade, as such, is consistent with this principle only if, indeed, comparable restrictions are extended to and applied in each market, each and every setting for potential voluntary exchange. But, if the restriction is so extended, no person in any market, as producer or consumer, will find such generalized restraint to be desirable. Agreement on a constitutionally enforced regime of free trade can, in this way, be derived from acceptance of the Rawlsian precept of the justice of equal liberty and the economic principle of mutual gains from exchange.

As a final note, I should emphasize that the argument and analysis just presented have been applied to the economics and welfare politics of a single national polity. The analysis, as such, makes no distinction between restrictions on the output of domestic producers and limits on supply to domestic markets by foreign producers. There has been no reference at all to the circumstances that describe markets for goods in other countries, since any such reference merely serves to confuse the discussion of the issues involved in free trade versus restricted trade. In the United States, restriction on the market for a single good, whether imposed on domestic or foreign suppliers, creates potential rents for *domestic* producers at the expense of *domestic* consumers. And this elementary logic holds quite independently of the state of the market, or markets, in other nations. I have tried here to suggest that these potential rents that producer interests seek to secure through market restraints may not be what they seem and that an analysis of the welfare politics may offer at least some grounds for hope of a constitutional restoration of a free trade regime both within and across national boundaries.

7. BETTER THAN PLOWING

Family Origins

MY TITLE's description of an academic career is taken directly from Frank H. Knight, from whom I take so much. Nonetheless, my origins in the rural agricultural poverty of the upper south (Tennessee) in the United States, along with the sometimes pretentious efforts of the middle-class poor to impose social distinctions, are surely explanatory elements in any narrative account of my history.

My family was poor, but, in the county, it was important. My grandfather, John P. Buchanan, was the county's only Governor of the State of Tennessee. He was a one-term phenomenon, having been elected as the nominee of the Farmers' Alliance Party, one of the several successful Populist electoral triumphs in 1891. By 1893, the Democratic Party had put its house in order, and the Populists had seen their best days. But Buchanan's governorship established the family in the community. The local public school which I attended for ten years was named "Buchanan School."

My father, the youngest of a large family, was responsible for the operation of the family farm after his siblings had departed. I grew up in a huge house on a hill, in varying states of disrepair, on a farm that had no owner. It was owned by "the Buchanan estate," which was not divided until the farm was sold in 1944, and long after I had entered military service. My father had no incentive for effective maintenance. He was a jack of all trades, a farmer, a some-

67

time carpenter, veterinarian, insulator, and equipment operator. He was locally political, a community Justice of the Peace during all of my childhood. A handsome man, he had been a fine athlete (two years varsity football at the University of Oklahoma); and with a fine sense of humor, he was a favorite with the ladies. He was possessed by intense personal courage; he made no pretense to intellectual interests.

My mother was the best and the brightest of a family of deputy sheriffs and Presbyterian preachers which had roughly the same class standing as my father's. As was general in rural Tennessee in the early years of this century, both families were pure Scots-Irish. My mother, Lila Scott, finished high school, took teacher training, and taught for a decade before meeting my father. Hers was the most curious mind I have known; she devoured anything she could find to read, and she was not discriminating, with interests ranging at least from Latin grammar through calculus through Zane Gray westerns. She, too, assumed easily a leadership role in the local community, organizing the parents' association for the school, rising rapidly to county and regional offices. But, for this narrative, she was my teacher, and beyond the teacher that is in all mothers. She advanced me two grades by home instruction, and helped me in assignments through college years.

Early Education

From my early years, I was assigned the role as family successor to my grandfather. I was to be lawyer-politician, and Vanderbilt University (pre-law, then law) was understood as the final rung on my educational ladder. There were early family misgivings about my personality; I did not exhibit the behavior of the exaggerated extrovert required for any budding politician. But law remained my career focus, and I was trained in public speaking. Economic reality destroyed this dream; Vanderbilt moved beyond the possible as the

Great Depression moved in. College was what I could afford, Middle Tennessee State Teachers' College in Murfreesboro, which allowed me to live at home and to earn enough for fees and books by milking dairy cows morning and night for four years.

My college education was non-systematic and stochastic. There was waste in the requirements in formal education, and poor instruction in biology, history, psychology, economics, and other subjects. But there was much of value in my exposure to Shakespeare, modern poetry, mathematics, and physics. When I finished, I had accumulated majors in three areas—mathematics, English literature, and social science, including economics. These college years were important as confidence builders; by the end of my second year my academic standing was the best in the college; the country boy more than held his own against the boys and girls from the towns.

Upon graduation in 1940, I faced three options—school teaching at $65 per month; employment in a Nashville bank at $75 per month, and a $50 per month fellowship in Economics at the University of Tennessee. My career as an economist was settled by the dominance of the third opportunity, not by any desire to save the world. The 1940–41 graduate year in Knoxville, Tennessee, helped me meet the world beyond. I learned no economics during that year, but I did learn about women and whiskey, which, after all, are important parts of an education. There were few good economists on the faculty, but I was exposed to a genuine scholar, a man whose work habits were important in shaping my own. Charles P. White became my example of the research economist, who took his position seriously and conveyed to me the notion that there is, after all, a moral element in academic employment. It was White also who, despite his own self-acknowledged limits in these respects, strongly advised me to stick with economic theory as the basis for all applications.

Plans were open beyond the one year until I secured a fellowship in Statistics at Columbia University for the 1941–42 academic year. But before I could take up this appointment, I was drafted into military service, and found myself in the United States Navy by August 1941.

I had an easy war. After officer training in New York, and a special stint at the Naval War college, I was assigned to the operations staff of Admiral C. W. Nimitz, Commander-in-Chief, Pacific Fleet. Aside from a six-weeks experience-gathering tour at sea during one of the island invasions, I worked throughout the war at Pearl Harbor and at Guam, at fleet headquarters control deep in the bowels of the earth. I enjoyed the military, the colleagues, the work, and the setting; and I was good at the job. For the first and only time in my life, I worked closely with men who were important in shaping the lives and destinies of many others. I saw these military leaders as ordinary mortals, trying to do their job within the constraints they faced, and burdened with their own prejudices like everyone else. This experience has helped me throughout my academic career; I have been able to relegate to the third order of smalls the sometime petty quarrels that seem to motivate professors everywhere, both in their roles as instructors and as research scholars.

In one sense my only career choice involved the decision to leave the navy and to return to civilian life. This decision was not easy; I knew the important persons, who urged me to stay; I had enjoyed the four years. But I made the correct choice, and was discharged in late 1945. With the GI government subsidy for further schooling available, and with a new wife for partial support, I considered alternative graduate schools. Columbia University no longer beckoned because New York City had not made me want to return. I knew nothing about the competence or the ideological makeup of the University of Chicago economics faculty. But a teacher from my undergraduate days at Middle Tennessee, with a Chicago Ph.D. in political science, conveyed to me the intellectual excitement of the place. Off to Chicago I went in late 1945, along with the many others who were just returning from military services.

Chicago, Frank Knight, and Knut Wicksell

Had I known about the ideological character of the Chicago faculty I might have chosen to go elsewhere. I was not overtly political or ideological in my salad days; emerging from the family populist tradition, I grew up in a solidly Democratic setting, with Roosevelt emerging as the popular leader in the 1930s. I was basically populist and pacifist. But officer training school in New York radicalized me. Along with many others, I was subjected to overt discrimination based on favoritism for products of the eastern establishment universities. This sobering experience made me forever sympathetic to those who suffer discriminatory treatment, and it forestalled any desire to be a part of any eastern establishment institution.

When I reached the University of Chicago, I was what I now best describe as a libertarian socialist. I had always been anti-state, anti-government, anti-establishment. But this included the establishment that controlled the United States economy. I had grown up on a reading diet from my grandfather's attic piled high with the radical pamphlets of the 1890s. The robber barons were very real to me.

At Chicago, I found myself no different from my graduate student colleagues, almost all of whom were socialist of one or another stripe. But within six weeks after enrollment in Frank Knight's course in price theory, I had been converted into a zealous advocate of the market order. Frank Knight was not an ideologue, and he made no attempt to convert anybody. But I was, somehow, ready for the understanding of economic process that his teaching offered. I was converted by the power of ideas, by an understanding of the model of the market. This experience shaped my attitude toward the use and purpose of economic instruction; if I could be converted so could others.

Frank Knight was *the* intellectual influence during my years at the University of Chicago, and his influence increased over subsequent years, enhanced by the development of a close personal relationship. Knight became my role model, without which I wonder what turns I might have taken. The qualities of mind that Knight exhibited were, and remain, those that I seek to emulate: the willingness to question anything, and anybody, on any subject anytime; the categorical refusal to accept anything as sacred; the genuine openness to all ideas; and finally, the basic conviction that most ideas peddled about are nonsense or worse when examined critically.

A second Chicago event profoundly affected my career. Having finished my work, including the German language examination, I had the leisure of a scholar without assignments in the Harper Library stacks during three months of the summer of 1948. By sheer chance, I pulled Knut Wicksell's 1896 dissertation on taxation from the shelves, a book that was untranslated and unknown. The effect on me was dramatic. Wicksell laid out before me a set of ideas that seemed to correspond precisely with those that I had already in my head, ideas that I could not have expressed and would not have dared to express in the public-finance mind-set of the time. Wicksell told us that if economists really want to apply the test of efficiency to the public sector, only the rule of unanimity for collective choice offers the procedural guarantee. If we seek reform in economic policy, we should change the rules under which political agents or representatives act. Economists should, once and for all, cease and desist proffering advice to nonexistent benevolent despots. Wicksell's were heady words, and from that day, I was determined to translate Wicksell's contribution into English.[1]

Visitors to my office know that photographs of only two economists grace the walls, Frank Knight and Knut Wicksell. I consider them co-equals, Knight in his influence on my attitudes toward the world of ideas generally, and Wicksell in his influence on the specific ideas that have come to be associated with my work

---

1. My translation of the centrally important part of the book was published in *Classics in the Theory of Public Finance* (1958).

in public choice and constitutional economics. Both of these influences were embedded in my psyche when I left Chicago in mid-1948.

I entered the highly competitive world of American academia with no conscious sense of intellectual direction. In one of my first articles, based in part on the Wicksell exposure and, in part, by reading a translation of De Viti De Marco, I called for a tie-in between the theory of the state and norms for taxation. The point seemed so simple, indeed obvious, yet so locked in was the utilitarian mind-set of orthodox public finance that the article was widely cited as seminal. In 1951, Kenneth Arrow published his widely heralded book on the general impossibility theorem. For three years, I was bemused by the failure of reviewers and critics to make the obvious point that the whole Arrow construction was inappropriate for a democratic society. Why should the social ordering satisfy consistency norms if individual values and preferences generated inconsistencies? I published a review article in 1954 that few economists understood then, or understand now. Almost as a footnote, I published a second short article comparing individual choice in voting and in the market. Again, the points made seemed simple, but surprisingly no one had made such a basic comparison. In those two papers, there were elements of much that was later to be developed in my contributions to public choice.

The two 1954 papers were published in the *Journal of Political Economy,* under the editorship of Earl J. Hamilton, who deserves special mention in this narrative. I had not taken his courses at the University of Chicago, and only in my last few months there did I get to know him personally. But we did establish a friendship, and from him I got the advice that one major key to academic success was to "deep the ass to the chair," a rule that I have followed and that I have passed along to several generations of students. But Hamilton's influence was not primarily in this piece of advice. Through his editorship of the journal, he encouraged rather than discouraged me as potential author; he was a tough editor, but his comments-reactions were never wholly negative, and it was only after several submissions that the two 1954 pieces were hammered into acceptable shape. Negation at that stage of my career might have been fatal.

The Italian Year

Hamilton was also influential in encouraging me to keep up with the languages, and I commenced to learn to read Italian. I wanted to go to Italy for a year's reading in the classical works in public finance theory. I got a Fullbright grant for the 1955–56 academic year, which I spent in Perugia and Rome. This Italian year was critical in the development of my ideas on the importance of the relationship between the political structure and the positive and normative theory of economic policy. The Italians had escaped the delusions of state omniscience and benevolence that had clouded the minds of England and German language social philosophers and scientists. The Italians had long since cut through the absurdities of Benthamite utilitarianism and Hegelian idealism. Real rather than idealized politics, with real persons as actors—these were the building blocks in the Italian construction, whether those of the cooperative-democratic state or the ruling class-monopoly state. Exposure to this Italian conceptualization of the state was necessary to enable me to break out of the idealistic-utilitarian mind-set that still imposes its intellectual straitjacket on many of my peers in social science. The Italian year was also important in the more general sense of offering insights into the distinctly non-American historical-cultural environment.

Public Debt and Opportunity Cost

The Italian research year was indirectly responsible for one strand of my work that may seem to represent a side alley, namely, my work in the theory of public debt, which was less successful in convincing my economist peers than other work in public choice and public finance. At the very end of the Italian year, I suddenly "saw the light." I realized that the whole conventional wisdom on public debt was simply wrong, and that the time had come for a restoration of the classical theory, which was correct in all its essentials. I was as excited by this personal discovery as I had been by the discovery of the Wicksell book almost a decade earlier. Immediately on my return to America in 1956, I commenced my first singly authored book, *Public Principles of Public Debt* (1958).

In my overall assessment, the work on public debt was not a digression. This work was simply another extension or application of what can be discerned as a central theme in my efforts from the very first papers written. I have been consistently reductionist in that I have insisted that analysis be factored down to the level of choices faced by individual actors. The orthodox theory of public debt that I challenged embodied a failure to treat relevant choice alternatives. My reasoning, once again, was simple. National economies, as such, cannot enjoy gains or suffer losses. The fact that making guns "uses up" resources in years of war tells us nothing at all about who must pay for those guns, and when. The whole macroaggregation exercise that had captured the attention of post-Keynesian economists was called into question.

My work on public debt stirred up considerable controversy in the early 1960s, and I realized that the ambiguity stemmed, in part, from an absence of clarity in my initial challenge. Confusion centered around the conception of opportunity cost, and I laid my plans to write a short book, which I consider my best work in economic theory, narrowly defined. This book, *Cost and Choice* (1969), again emphasizes my central theme, the reduction of analysis to individual choice settings which, in this extension, implies the necessity of defining cost in utility rather than commodity dimensions.

Gordon Tullock, *The Calculus of Consent,* and Public Choice

I first encountered Gordon Tullock in 1958, when he came to the University of Virginia as a postdoctoral research fellow. I was impressed by his imagination and originality, and by his ability to recognize easily the elements of my own criticism of public debt orthodoxy. Tullock insisted not only that analysis be reduced to individual choice but, also, that individuals be modeled always as maximizers of self-interest, a step that I had sometimes been unwilling to take, despite my exposure to the Italians. Tullock wrote his seminal paper on the working of simple majority rule, and we decided to collaborate on a book that would examine the individual's choice among alternative political rules. We more or less explicitly considered our exercise to be an implicit defense of the Madisonian structure embodied in the United States Constitution.

The Calculus of Consent (1962) was the first work in what we now call "constitutional economics," and it achieved the status of a "classic" in public choice theory. In retrospect, it is interesting, to me, that there was no sense of "discovery" at any point in that book's construction, no moment of excitement akin to those accompanying either the discovery of the Wicksell book or the insight into public debt theory. Tullock and I considered ourselves to be applying relatively simple economic analysis to the choice among alternative political decision rules, with more or less predictable results. We realized that no one had attempted to do precisely what we were doing, but the exercise was essentially one of "writing out the obvious" rather than opening up wholly new areas for inquiry.

We were wrong. Public choice, as a subdiscipline in its own right, emerged in the early 1960s, in part from the reception of our book, in part from our own organizational-entrepreneurial efforts which later emerged in the Public Choice Society, in part from other works. Once the whole complex web of political decision rules and procedures was opened up for economic analysis, the range of application seemed open-ended. Public choice, in the 1960s was both exciting and easy; it is not surprising that graduate students in our program at Virginia were highly successful and that budding economists and political scientists quickly latched onto the new subdiscipline.[2]

My own work does not exhibit a dramatic switching to public choice economics from standard public finance. As I have noted above, from my earliest papers I had emphasized the importance of political structure, a conviction that was strengthened by my exposure to the Italians. Immediately after my excursion into the theory of public debt and before collaboration with Tullock on *The Calculus of Consent*, I wrote a long survey essay on the Italian tradition in public finance and published this essay, along with other pieces, in *Fiscal Theory and Political Economy* (1960). Considered as a package, my work over the decade, 1956–66, involved filling in gaps in the taxonomy of public goods theory along with various attempts to factor down familiar propositions in theoretical welfare economics into individualized choice settings. The paper "Externality" (1962), written jointly with W. C. Stubblebine, was an amalgamation of strands of argument from Wicksell, Coase, and Pigou. The paper "An Economic Theory of Clubs" (1965) was a filling in of an obvious gap in the theory of public goods.

During the early 1960s, my work specifically shifted toward an attempt to tie two quasi-independent strands of inquiry together, those of orthodox public finance and the theory of political decision structure. The result was a relatively neglected book, *Public Finance*

---

2. For two volumes devoted largely to applications, see James M. Buchanan and Robert Tollison (Eds.), *Theory of Public Choice* (1972), and *Theory of Public Choice, II* (1984).

in Democratic Process (1967), which contained implications for normative theory that remain unrecognized by modern research scholars.

The research program embodied in elementary public choice theory developed almost naturally in a sequence of applications to the theory of economic policy. The whole of the Keynesian and post-Keynesian theory of macroeconomic management (including monetarism) depends critically on the presumption that political agents respond to considerations of "public interest" rather than to the incentives imposed upon them by constituents. Once these agents are modeled as ordinary persons, the whole policy structure crumbles. This basic public choice critique of the Keynesian theory of policy was presented in *Democracy in Deficit* (1977), written jointly with Richard E. Wagner. I have often used the central argument of this book as the clearest example of the applicability of elementary public choice theory, the implications of which have been corroborated in the accumulating evidence provided by the regime of quasi-permanent budget deficits.

Between Anarchy and Leviathan

Through the middle 1960s, my analysis and interpretation of the workings of democratic politics were grounded in a relatively secure belief that, despite the many political failures that public choice theory allows us to identify, ultimately the governing authorities, as constrained by constitutional structure, respond to and implement the values and preferences of individual citizens. This belief in the final efficacy of democratic process surely affected my analysis, even if unconsciously, and allowed me to defend the essential "logic" of political institutions in being against the sometime naive proposals made by social reformers.

This foundational belief was changed by the events of the late

1960s. I lost my "faith" in the effectiveness of government as I observed the explosive take-off in spending rates and new programs, engineered by self-interested political agents and seemingly divorced from the interests of citizens. At the same time, I observed what seemed to me to be a failure of the institutional structure, at all levels, to respond effectively to mounting behavioral disorder. The United States government seemed to take on aspects of an agent-driven Leviathan simultaneously with the emergence of anarchy in civil society.

What was happening, and how could my explanatory model be applied to the modified reality of the late 1960s and early 1970s? I sensed the necessity of plunging much deeper into basic political philosophy than heretofore, and I found it useful to examine more closely the predicted operating properties in both anarchy and Leviathan. I was fortunate in that I located colleagues who assisted and greatly complemented my efforts in each case. Winston C. Bush formalized the anarchy of the Hobbesian jungle in terms of modern economic theory. Bush's independent and foundational analysis provided me with the starting point for the book that remains the most coherent single statement of my research program, *The Limits of Liberty* (1975).

Although chapters in that book raised the threat of the Leviathan state, I had not worked out the formal analysis. Again I was lucky to be able to work with Geoffrey Brennan in pushing along this frontier of inquiry. We commenced the exciting project that emerged as *The Power to Tax* (1980). That book explored the implications of the hypothesis that government maximizes revenues from any taxing authority constitutionally granted to it. Such analysis seems required for any informed constitutional calculus involving a grant of taxing power to government. As reviewers noted, the result of our analysis here was to stand much of the conventional wisdom in normative tax theory on its head.

Constitutionalism and the Social Contract

As I noted earlier, *The Calculus of Consent* (1962) was the first explicit contribution in the research program that we now call "constitutional economics" or "constitutional political economy." Gordon Tullock and I were analyzing the individual's choice among alternative rules for reaching political decisions, rules to which he, along with others, would be subject in subsequent periods of operation. Such a choice setting is necessarily different in kind from that normally treated by economists, which is the choice among end objects within well-defined constraints. In a very real sense, the choice among rules becomes a choice among constraints, and, hence, involves a higher-state calculus of decision than that which most economists examine.

We were initially influenced to analyze the choice among political rules by at least two factors that I can now identify. First, we were dissatisfied by the apparent near-universal and unquestioned acceptance of majority rule as the ideal for collective decision processes. Secondly, we were influenced by our then colleague Rutledge Vining, himself an early student of Frank Knight, who hammered home to all who would listen that economic policy choices are not made among allocations or distributions, but are, necessarily, among rules or institutions that generate patterns of allocations and distributions. Vining's emphasis was on the stochastic nature of these patterns of outcomes and on the necessity for an appreciation for and understanding of the elementary theory of probability.

How does a person choose among the rules to which he will be subject? Vining took from Knight, and passed along to me, a fully sympathetic listener, the analogy with the choice of rules in ordinary games, from poker to basketball. The chooser, at the rule-choosing or constitutional stage of deliberation cannot identify how any particular rule will precisely affect his own position in subsequent rounds of play. Who can know how the cards will fall? The choice among rules is, therefore, necessarily made under what we should now call a "veil of uncertainty." *The Calculus of Consent* was our straightforward extension of this nascent research program to the game of politics.

In constitutional choice there is no well-defined maximand analogous to that which describes garden-variety economic choice. The individual may still be modeled as a utility maximizer, but there is no readily available means of arraying alternatives. The formal properties of choice under uncertainty, properties that have been exhaustively explored during the middle decades of this century, did not concern us. But we did sense the positive value of the uncertainty setting in opening up the potential for agreement on rules. If an individual cannot know how specific rules will affect his own position, he will be led to choose among rules in accordance with some criterion of generality rather than particularly. And if all persons reason similarly, the prospects for some Wicksellian-like agreement on rules are much more favorable than prospects for agreement on political choices to be made within a defined rules structure. In my own interpretation, in *The Calculus of Consent*, Tullock and I were shifting the Wicksellian unanimity norm for efficiency in collective choice from the in-period level, where its limits are severe, to the constitutional level where no comparable limits are present.

This construction in *The Calculus of Consent* was essentially worked out independently of the comparable construction of John Rawls. But discovery of his early paper on "Justice as Fairness" during the course of writing our book served to give us confidence that we were on a reasonable track. As early as the late 1950s, Rawls had spelled out his justice-as-fairness criterion and had introduced early versions of his veil of ignorance, which was to become universally familiar after the publication of his acclaimed treatise, *A Theory of Justice* (1971). The coincidence both in the timing of our initial work and in the basic similarity in analytical constructions has made me share an affinity with Rawls that has seemed mysterious to critics of both of us.

The subject matter of economics has always seemed to me to be the institution of exchange, embodying agreement between or among choosing parties. The Wicksellian extension of the exchange paradigm to the many-person collective has its most direct application in the theory of public finance, but when applied to the choice among political rules the analysis moves into areas of inquiry that are foreign to economists. At this research juncture, the disciplinary base merges into political philosophy, and the exchange paradigm becomes a natural component of a general contractarian theory of political interaction. Almost by definition, the economist who shifts his attention to political process while retaining his methodological individualism must be contractarian.

As noted earlier, my emphasis has been on factoring down complex interactions into individual choice components and, where possible, to explain and interpret such interactions in terms of cooperation rather than conflict models. Interpersonal, intergroup, and interparty conflict can scarcely be left out of consideration when we examine ordinary politics within defined constitutional structures. The contractarian or exchange program must shift, almost by necessity, to the stage of choice among rules. The contractarian becomes a constitutionalist, and I have often classified my own position with both these terms.

I have continued to be surprised at the reluctance of my colleagues in the social sciences, and especially in economics, to share the contractarian-constitutionalist research program and to understand the relevance of looking at politics and governance in terms of the two-stage decision process. A substantial share of my work over the decade, 1975–1985, involved varying attempts to persuade my peers to adopt the constitutional attitude. In two volumes of collected essays, *Freedom in Constitutional Contract* (1978), and *Liberty,*

Market, and State (1985), as well as in a book jointly with Geoffrey Brennan, *The Reason of Rules* (1985), I sought to defend the contractarian-constitutionalist methodology in many applications.

Academic Exit and Virginia Political Economy

Both in response to the demands of the series of autobiographical essays in which this paper appears and to my own preferences, I have, aside from the first two background sections, concentrated on the intellectual record, on the development of the ideas that have characterized my work, and on the persons and events that seem to have affected these ideas. I have deliberately left out of account the details of my personal, private experiences over the course of a long career. My essay would, however, be seriously incomplete if I should neglect totally the influences of the academic-intellectual environments within which I have been able to pursue my work, including the stimulation I have secured from colleagues, staff, and students, whose names are not entered in these accounts.

I cannot, of course, test what "might have been" had I chosen academic settings other than I did select. I feel no acute sense of opportunities missed, nor do I classify any choices made as having been grossly mistaken. I have exercised the academic exit option that the competitive structure of the United States academy offers. In so doing, I have reduced the ability of those who might have sought to modify the direction of my research and teaching efforts, while, at the same time, I have secured the benefits from the unintended consequences that shifts in location always guarantee.

This much said, I would be remiss if I did not include some form of tribute to the three academic settings within Virginia that have provided me with professional breathing space for almost all of my career. Mr. Jefferson's "academical village," the University of Virginia, where I spent twelve years, 1956–1968, allowed Warren Nutter and me full rein in establishing the Thomas Jefferson Center for Studies in Political Economy. This Center, as an institution, encouraged me and others to counter the increasing technical specialization of economics and, for me, to keep the subject matter interesting when the discipline, in more orthodox hands, threatened to become boring in the extreme. Virginia Polytechnic Institute, or VPI, where I spent fourteen years, 1969–1983, allowed Charles Goetz, Gordon Tullock, and me to organize the Center for Study of Public Choice, a Center that became, for a period in the 1979s and early 1980s, an international haven for research scholars who sought some exposure to the blossoming new subdiscipline of public choice. Finally, George Mason University, to which the whole Center shifted in 1983, insured a continuity in my research emphasis and tradition, even beyond that of my active career.

Retrospective

Other contributors to this series have discussed the influences on their developments as "economists." I am not at all sure that I qualify for inclusion in terms of this professional or disciplinary classification. I am not, and have never been, an "economist" in any narrowly defined meaning. My interest in understanding how the economic interaction process works has always been instrumental to the more inclusive purpose of understanding how we can learn to live one with another without engaging in Hobbesian war and without subjecting ourselves to the dictates of the state. The "wealth of nations," as such, has never commanded my attention save as a valued by-product of an effectively free society. The ways and means through which the social order might be made more "efficient" in the standard meaning—these orthodox guidelines have carried relatively little weight for me.

Neither have I considered myself a "pure scientist" and my work as "pure science." I have not been engaged in some exciting quest for discovery of a reality that exists independently of our own making. I have sensed acutely the exhilaration in ideas that is shared by all scientists in the broader meaning, but the ideas that capture my attention are those that, directly or indirectly, explain how freely choosing individuals can secure jointly desired goals. The simple exchange of apples and oranges between two traders—this institutional model is the starting point for all that I have done. Contrast this with the choice between apples and oranges in the utility-maximizing calculus of Robinson Crusoe. The second model is the starting point for most of what most economists do.

If this difference between my foundational model and that of other economists is recognized, my work takes on an internal coherence and consistency that may not be apparent absent such recognition. The coherence was not, of course, a deliberately chosen element of a research program. I have written largely in response to ideas that beckoned, ideas that offered some intellectual challenge and that had not, to my knowledge, been developed by others. I have rarely been teased by either the currency of policy topics or the fads of academic fashion, and when I have been so tempted my work has suffered. The coherence that the work does possess stems from the simple fact that I have worked from a single methodological perspective during the four decades that span my career to date, along with the fact that I have accepted the normative implications of this perspective. The methodological perspective and the normative stance are shared by few of my peers in modern social science. This location of my position outside the mainstream has the inestimable value of providing me with the continuing challenge to seek still other ideas and applications that may, ultimately, shift the frontier of effective agreement outward.

ABOUT THE AUTHOR

James McGill Buchanan received a Ph.D. in economics from the University of Chicago in 1948. During World War II, he was an officer of the United States Navy on the operations staff of Admiral Nimitz at Pearl Harbor. A Distinguished Fellow of the American Economic Association, Professor Buchanan received the Nobel Memorial Prize in Economic Science in 1986 for his contributions to public finance, political economy, and the theory of public choice. He is currently Harris University Professor at George Mason University, Fairfax, Virginia.

Production Notes

This book was designed by Roger Eggers. Composition and paging were done on the Quadex Composing System and typesetting on the Compugraphic 8400 by the design and production staff of University of Hawaii Press.

The text and display typeface is Compugraphic Bembo.

Offset presswork and binding were done by Vail-Ballou Press, Inc. Text paper is Glatfelter Offset Vellum, basis 50.